UNFINISHED BUSINESS

Unfinished Business

An American Strategy for Iraq Moving Forward

Kenneth M. Pollack

Raad Alkadiri

J. Scott Carpenter

Frederick W. Kagan

Sean Kane

With contributions from
Joost Hiltermann

BROOKINGS INSTITUTION PRESS
Washington, D.C.

A SABAN CENTER AT THE BROOKINGS INSTITUTION BOOK
Originally released as Analysis Paper 22, December 2010

Library of Congress Cataloging-in-Publication data is available

ISBN: 978-0-8157-2165-9 (pbk. : alk. paper)

9 8 7 6 5 4 3 2 1

Printed on acid-free paper

Typeset in Sabon

Composition by Cynthia Stock
Silver Spring, Maryland

Printed by R. R. Donnelley
Harrisonburg, Virginia

Contents

Preface

Unfinished Business: An American Strategy for Iraq Moving Forward is the product of a remarkable transformation. Not the transformation of Iraq, but the transformation of the views of analysts in the United States who work on Iraq. During the spring of 2010, in the midst of Iraq's post-election wrangling, the six members of this group met on several occasions at small dinners and other meetings related to Iraq. Over the course of those gatherings we realized that although many of us had once differed vociferously in our views regarding American policy toward Iraq, our disagreements had abated rather dramatically. Indeed, there seemed to be a surprising convergence in our thinking despite our widely differing political backgrounds.

In response, during the late summer and early fall of 2010, Kenneth Pollack of the Saban Center for Middle East Policy at the Brookings Institution convened the group formally as a working group on Iraq. Unfortunately, Frederick Kagan of the American Enterprise Institute was asked to come to Afghanistan by General Stanley McChrystal to help the U.S. military with that mission. As a result, Fred had to follow our activities remotely, via emails, written notes from the sessions, and the odd face-to-face meeting whenever he was in town. The rest of us spent long hours together hashing out every significant issue related to Iraq and U.S. policy toward Iraq. In the end, there were still some differences among us, but the degree of consensus—and consensus on a number of rather bold statements about what the United States will need to do to secure its interests in Iraq in the future—was remarkable. By the end of our conversations, members of our group who had once been ready to do great violence to one another over their differences found themselves in violent agreement over what needed to be done. The product of that harmonic convergence is this report.

Joost Hiltermann of the International Crisis Group attended most of our meetings, participated fully in the conversations, and contributed a number of important ideas to the final product.

As for the rest of us, the views expressed in these pages are ours alone and do not constitute the positions of the American Enterprise Institute, the Brookings Institution, PFC Energy, the United States Institute of Peace, or the Washington Institute for Near East Policy.

We were extremely fortunate to have the advice of a remarkable collection of people. Ambassador Ryan Crocker, Lt. General James Dubik (ret.), Ambassador Charles Reis, and Emma Sky were all exceptionally generous with their time, experience, and expertise. They provided comments on an early draft of this report and their insights made this a far better product than it otherwise would have been. We are deeply grateful to them for their wisdom. In addition, Bob Cassily of the U.S. State Department shared the fruits of his experience with the Provincial Reconstruction Teams in Iraq with us, which proved invaluable to key sections of this report. Any and all remaining mistakes or stupid ideas are ours alone.

Kenneth M. Pollack
Raad Alkadiri
J. Scott Carpenter
Frederick W. Kagan
Sean Kane

UNFINISHED BUSINESS

INTRODUCTION

Iraq still hangs in the balance. The dramatic improvements in Iraqi security between 2007 and 2009 have produced important, but incomplete changes in Iraq's politics. These changes make it possible to imagine Iraq slowly muddling upward, building gradually toward a better future.

However, Americans must be constantly on guard against the considerable potential for Iraq to slip into all-out civil war. There are dozens of scenarios—from military coups, to official misconduct, to the assassination of one or two key leaders—that could spark such violence. The conflict might look somewhat different than before, perhaps featuring Arab-Kurd conflict, greater intra-Shi'i fighting, or various parts of the Iraqi security forces warring for control of the state.

Iraq's own internal dynamics and the history of intercommunal civil wars indicate that if Iraq does not find a way to muddle slowly upward toward greater stability, it is far more likely that it will slide quickly backward into the chaos of all-out civil war than that it would simply muddle downward toward an unpleasant, weak, but minimally stable state that need not concern the United States.

Washington has signaled its intention to withdraw U.S. military forces from the country, sooner rather than later. What is not clear, however, is what the United States hopes to accomplish before its troops depart and its other resources attenuate, or how it plans to reach its goals. Washington has announced a strategy to exit, but it has not yet formulated an exit strategy that will secure and sustain American interests in Iraq and the region.

Although U.S. influence in Iraq remains substantial, it is less than what it has been in the past. It is diminishing as American troops leave Iraq, as American resources are diverted elsewhere, and as the Iraqis themselves regain the ability to secure their country and govern themselves. This makes it all the more imperative that the United States have a clear strategic concept that establishes clear goals and well-defined objectives that can be achieved with this reduced panoply of tools.

PRIORITIES OF AN EXIT STRATEGY

An American strategy for exiting Iraq must include a ruthless prioritization of U.S. goals and objectives to ensure that the United States directs its residual influence toward securing, first, what is absolutely vital, and only then whatever else is possible.

The United States will have several different goals as it exits Iraq, but these goals, and the objectives they imply, are not all of equal importance, and Washington must recognize the priorities among them. The following should be the priority for U.S. interests in Iraq:

—*Iraq cannot be allowed to descend back into civil war.* Because of Iraq's own resources and its position in the economically vital and geo-strategically sensitive Persian Gulf region, it would be disastrous for American vital national interests if Iraq were to slip into an all-out civil war, which still remains very possible.

—*Iraq cannot reemerge as an aggressive state.* There is little danger of this in the near term, but as the United States works to build a strong, cohesive Iraq that would not relapse into internal conflict, it also must avoid building one that is so powerful and self-confident that it will threaten its neighbors.

—*Iraq should ideally be a strong, prosperous U.S. ally.* Because it will be difficult enough to ensure that Iraq averts civil war and does not emerge as a new "Frankenstein's monster" of the Gulf, this last objective should be seen as an aspirational goal rather than an irreducible necessity.

WHAT AMERICA'S OVERALL STRATEGY SHOULD BE

Since Iraq is now a fully sovereign nation enjoying a resurgence of nationalism, it is essential that Iraqis see themselves as benefiting from continued American involvement in Iraq. The more the Iraqis believe that the relationship with the United States is of value to them, the more desirous they will be of preserving ties to the United States, and the more willing they will be to overlook American interference or see it as positive, and the more afraid they will be of losing those ties. In this respect, Iraqis generally desire continued American aid, investment, and technical assistance, as well as U.S. help regaining Iraq's full international standing by resolving major diplomatic issues that arose from Saddam Husayn's misdeeds.

The Strategic Framework Agreement (SFA), a partnership document between Iraq and the United States that was initiated by the Iraqi government, provides a foundation for this type of assistance. If the United States wants to maintain leverage in Iraq, the SFA must ultimately deliver outcomes that Iraqis value.

For these same reasons, the United States must work in tandem with the United Nations Assistance Mission for Iraq, other international organizations, and its allies (in the region, in Europe, and elsewhere) more than ever before. The more that the United States can move in synch with the UN and American allies, the more palatable American initiatives will be to Iraqis.

The most important source of American influence moving forward is conditionality. Virtually all American assistance needs to be conditioned on Iraqis doing the things that the United States needs them to do, which in every case is likely to be something that is in the long-term interests of the Iraqi people and the Iraqi nation, albeit not necessarily in the short-term interests of various Iraqi politicians. Conditioning assistance means linking specific aspects of American activities to specific, related aspects of Iraqi behavior. It also means tying wider aspects of American cooperation with Iraq to the general course of the Iraqi political system.

Ultimately, the United States must condition the continuation of the U.S.-Iraqi relationship on the willingness of the Iraqi political leadership to guide their country in the direction of greater stability, inclusivity, and effective governance.

Vital American Interests: Politics

Iraq's domestic politics has become the center of gravity of the American effort toward Iraq. The future of Iraq will be determined principally by the course of its domestic politics, and that in turn will determine whether America's vital interests there are safeguarded.

— *If Iraq's domestic political framework collapses, so too will its security.* Security in Iraq has improved significantly, but it will only hold over the long term if Iraqi politics sorts itself out.

— *If the Iraqi economy collapses, it will almost certainly stem from a failure of Iraq's domestic politics.* Iraq's economy continues to sputter along and it will only improve when there is a government in Baghdad able to govern effectively.

Because Iraq's domestic politics is the key to the future stability of the country, and because it remains so fragile, it must be the principal American focus as the United States diminishes its involvement in Iraq. The absolute highest priority for the United States during the ongoing drawdown and for the next several years must be to see Iraq's domestic politics work out properly.

Specifically, this will mean that several important standards must be met: continuing progress on democracy, transparency, and the rule of law; continued development of bureaucratic capacity; no outbreak of revolutionary activity, including coups d'état; no emergence of dictators; reconciliation among the various ethno-sectarian groupings, as well as within them; a reasonable delineation of center-periphery relations, including a workable agreement over the nature of federalism; and an equitable management and distribution of Iraq's oil wealth, as well as the overall economic prosperity that must result from such distribution.

Moreover, the United States cannot be confident that its paramount objectives of preventing civil war/instability in Iraq have been fully secured until the Iraqis have appropriately addressed the remaining problems in the Iraqi Constitution because these threaten the viability of the state. It would be fundamentally irresponsible for the United States to assume that the Iraqis will be able to overcome the gaps in the Constitution to achieve a stable polity without outside support.

Supporting Iraq's Political Development

Unfortunately, domestic politics may well prove to be the one area where Iraq's political leadership will stop at nothing to keep the United States out. Iraq's political leaders have a less than stellar record of obeying the rules of the new political game, and the United States continues to provide the ultimate insurance that no group will be able to completely overturn the system and dominate others. This is a U.S. role that many Iraqis continue to regard as at least a necessary evil if not a positive good. Thus, it is important for both the future of Iraq and for America's vital interests that the United States focus its energy and resources on Iraq's domestic politics.

To maximize its ability to influence Iraq's domestic politics, the United States must be prepared to subordinate virtually every other aspect of its Iraq policy by making major sacrifices in areas previously held sacrosanct. Almost every other element of the U.S.-Iraq relationship needs to be seen as leverage to get the Iraqis to do what is necessary in the one area of greatest importance to the United States (and to their own long-term best interests as well).

Although the United States has vital national interests invested in the future of Iraq, it would be a mistake for Washington to determine that it will remain committed to Iraq under any and all circumstances. As long as Iraq's leaders are moving their country in the direction that serves American interests, the United States can and should remain willing to help the Iraqis generously.

However, the United States must acknowledge that the Iraqis may choose not to move in that direction. Many Iraqi leaders resist the rule of law, constitutional limits, and other constraints when it does not suit their own narrow interests. They may regard America's role in Iraq as a hindrance to their acting as they please.

If Iraq's leaders are *not* willing or able to act in a manner consistent with good governance, the rule of law, and the need for national reconciliation, then the risks to Iraq's future stability are so grave that they should cause the U.S. government to reevaluate its level of commitment to the U.S.-Iraqi partnership and the resources it is willing to invest in it.

VITAL AMERICAN INTERESTS: SECURITY

At present, all American troops are scheduled to depart Iraq by December 31, 2011, when the current Security Agreement between Iraq and the United States expires. Nevertheless, there are clear potential security and political benefits of a continued American military presence in Iraq after that date. In the near term, a continued presence of U.S. troops is likely to help sustain Iraq's recent security gains and provide some insurance and confidence that basic rules of the political system will be respected.

Yet, it is not the case that maintaining an American military presence in Iraq is so compelling that it should override all other considerations. From the U.S. perspective, retaining American troops in Iraq makes sense only if those troops have sufficient authority and capability to secure America's interest in a stable Iraq. Thus, conditionality must also govern whether the United States maintains a continuing military presence in Iraq.

This is clearly a topic of great sensitivity to Iraqis. A continuing U.S. troop presence will only be broadly accepted if it is perceived as being requested by Iraqis, negotiated in a transparent manner between the U.S. and Iraqi governments, and approved by Iraq's Parliament.

Prioritizing Missions

In the past, American military forces in Iraq have taken on a wide range of missions both because Iraq needed them to and because there were sufficient numbers available to enable them to do so. Today, both circumstances have changed. Consequently, in the military sphere, it is especially pressing that the United States engage in the same ruthless prioritization that it must apply across the board when formulating a strategy for its relationship with Iraq in the future.

Those priorities must be driven by *American* interests in Iraq moving forward. However, this principle cannot be applied myopically: some U.S. military missions are critical to American interests because they directly bolster America's paramount interest in preventing a civil war. Others, however, may be equally important because they indirectly support the same interests by providing a source of leverage over Iraqi domestic politics—the principal determinant of Iraqi stability or instability for the foreseeable future.

Flowing from the preeminent American interest in preventing an internal crisis that could trigger an all-out civil war, by far the most important U.S. military mission now is to support Iraq's internal stability by continuing to perform peacekeeping functions especially, but not exclusively, in Kirkuk and other territories disputed by Arabs and Kurds in northern Iraq. Used correctly, U.S. troops can be a crucial substitute for the trust that undergirds stable societies. Rebuilding trust in Iraq, as in all societies broken by intercommunal strife, will take years, and in the meantime, the Iraqis need some powerful external force to reassure them that their rivals (including rivals in the government) will not be able to use force against them. Realistically, that external force can only be the U.S. military.

A mission that once was of preeminent importance to the United States in Iraq that can now be assigned a much lower priority is counterterrorism. Terrorism in Iraq is no longer a threat to Iraqi stability—although if this were to change, so should its corresponding priority for American forces.

Similarly, the United States will have to rethink its willingness to accept risks to its personnel. Washington cannot ignore force protection, but neither can it make it the highest priority of American forces in Iraq.

The president's decision to draw down forces from Iraq relatively quickly means accepting risk because it will be impossible for the remaining U.S. forces to continue to fulfill all of the tasks they have in the past, to the same extent as in the past, and with the same safety tolerances. The remaining troops and civilians will have to complete those missions critical to U.S. vital interests and because there will be fewer of them with fewer resources at their disposal, this task will be extremely difficult. It would be impossible for the remaining U.S. military personnel to pursue American interests if force protection were to become their highest priority.

A New Agreement with Iraq

It is hard to imagine that Iraq will progress so rapidly that all American troops could be responsibly withdrawn by the end of 2011, according to the timetable of the current U.S.-Iraq Security Agreement (SA). It seems far more likely that several thousands—perhaps even tens of thousands—will still be needed for several years more, although the exact duration is impossible to say because it should be governed by the maturation of the Iraqi political process. This means that the United States and Iraq will need to come to an agreement on a new status of forces agreement (SOFA) to follow the expiration of the current SA.

The United States cannot want a new status of forces agreement more than the Iraqis want it themselves. There are three crucial, inter-related rules the United States should observe when negotiating a new SOFA with Iraq:

1. The United States must have a new SOFA with Iraq that preserves the ability of American forces to serve as peacekeepers and as the ultimate guardian of Iraqi rule of law.

2. The Iraqis must understand that the entire U.S. military, political, economic, and diplomatic aid relationship with Iraq is tied to the signing of a new SOFA that meets American needs.

3. The United States must be ready to walk away from Iraq altogether if the government of Iraq is unwilling to agree to such a SOFA.

VITAL AMERICAN INTERESTS: GOVERNANCE AND ECONOMICS

It is no longer a vital American interest to make an across-the-board effort to rebuild Iraq's economy and governmental apparatus. Progress on governance and economics has largely switched from being something that the United States required the Iraqis to do for American interests, to something that the Iraqis need American help doing for their own interests. One reason for this is that better governmental and economic performance is now something that the Iraqi leadership needs in order to maintain its own legitimacy and hold on power.

The consolidation of a stable, democratic Iraq depends in particular upon the evolution of a government that is seen as legitimate and effective, and the development of an economy that provides opportunities and livelihoods to Iraq's young and fast-growing population. After the provision of basic security, the two most critical standards by which the political system will be judged are the delivery of essential services, especially electricity, and increased employment.

The fundamental governance and economic challenge in Iraq is to improve the efficiency and transparency of the processes that transform a barrel of oil sold into the goods and services that the Iraqi public desires—like increased electricity output, water and sewage networks, roads, schools, health clinics, and job opportunities.

U.S. economic and governance assistance to Iraq should therefore be conditioned upon the Iraqi authorities putting in place oversight and accountability mechanisms aimed at limiting the corrupting and insulating effects of Iraq's oil economy.

The central challenge in this area will be reconciling U.S. and Iraqi expectations for future American aid and finding creative ways to use the SFA and whatever assistance the Congress and the administration are willing to make available in an era of sharply declining resources. The United States will need to be upfront with the Iraqi government that it cannot expect a new Marshall Plan for Iraq and that Washington will only be making relatively limited additional financial contributions to Iraq's reconstruction.

Fortunately, there are key areas of the Iraqi economy where U.S. diplomatic support, technical assistance, consulting services, and technology and knowledge transfers could deliver substantial economic and even political benefits to Iraq's new government. These should all be used as leverage to push for greater transparency in Iraqi governance.

CHAPTER ONE

GOALS AND INFLUENCE

America is not finished in Iraq. Not in any sense of the word. American interests in Iraq have not yet been secured, and so the United States will probably remain deeply engaged in Iraq for years to come. America's influence there may have abated, but it is far from spent. Indeed, the United States remains one of the most influential actors in Iraq, although that influence will only remain if Washington learns to wield it more skillfully.

President Obama warned "that we have not seen the end of American sacrifice in Iraq" and stressed that he wants to bring the Iraq war to a "responsible end."[1] The hard, incongruous truth is that a responsible American exit from Iraq has to be everything the hasty and ill-planned 2003 U.S. invasion was not. The United States may have stepped back from combat operations, but it has yet to fully define a strategy for achieving a long-term partnership with Iraq that can serve core American interests and help Iraq's fledgling democracy avoid a slide back to civil war. Under certain circumstances and with Iraqi concurrence, this would require extensive American engagement with Iraq for many years. Under other circumstances, America should be prepared to simply walk away if Iraqi leaders take steps directly inimical to U.S. interests and their own country's stability.

Meanwhile, the United States remains a key enabler of the Iraqi government and military, and there are a wide range of technical, economic, diplomatic, and security benefits that Iraq desires in a long-term partnership with the world's sole superpower. Moreover, the situation in Iraq no longer resonates as broadly in U.S. domestic politics as it once did, giving this and future administrations greater room to exercise conditionality in the U.S.-Iraqi relationship. What is now required is a carefully considered and pragmatic plan to wield these sources of influence in pursuit of a ruthlessly prioritized set of fundamental goals. This is the essence of partnership—it must serve the interests of both sides.

The Uncertain Future of Iraq

After American missteps in 2003–2006 pushed Iraq into a sectarian war that threatened to consume the country altogether, the array of changes often referred to by the shorthand of the "surge" stabilized the country and pulled Iraq back from the brink of the abyss. Further refinements to American strategy and tactics, the maturation of Iraq's security forces, and the emergence of an Iraqi leadership willing to take bold action on security matters then enabled U.S. and Iraqi forces to fill the security vacuum that had given rise to the internecine conflict in the first place, break the stranglehold of the militias, and bring real security to most of the country.

The dramatic improvements in Iraqi security between 2007 and 2009 have produced important, but incomplete changes in Iraq's politics. Democracy, in its most rudimentary form, has broken out. Iraqi leaders must wheel and deal for votes—from voters, from parliamentarians, and even from cabinet members within the government itself. It is a frustrating experience for former warlords, revolutionaries, tribal shaykhs, and clergymen, but they are learning. In addition to the new incentive structure that democracy has introduced to

Iraqi politics, Baghdad has also seen the reemergence of Iraq's more traditional and less enlightened forms of politics. Ethnic, religious, and tribal differences compete with democratic pressures. Personal charisma and personal animosities remain critical factors in the political direction of the country, and fear, conspiracies, and extra-constitutional practices remain all too common.

Unfortunately, while the security situation has improved, the United States has missed important opportunities to consolidate and accelerate Iraq's political evolution. The surge was meant in part to create a breathing space for Iraqi factions to address the most pressing disputes that continue to be a source of lasting tension and that threaten stability in the longer term. It was also meant to change the incentives of Iraq's leaders, by depriving them of violence as a tool and giving the Iraqi people the standing to demand positive changes without fear. In part because the United States has not held Iraq's leaders' feet to the fire and in part because the United States at times pushed for the wrong things, many have been able to consolidate their own narrow hold on power, evading key political reforms and retarding the democratic transformation.

Today, the United States has less leverage to push for reform because Washington has put security priorities above political change and provided Iraqi leaders with an excuse to consolidate the status quo. In doing so, the United States has also allowed Iran to regain considerable influence in Iraq after the surge had temporarily marginalized Tehran's influence. As a result, Iran continues to play a sharply destabilizing role in Iraq by supporting a host of violent groups across the political spectrum and ruthlessly promoting its own interests in Baghdad by making sectarianism—and Shi'i ascendency—the framework for a new government. Tehran therefore threatens to erase the progress witnessed over the past two years. In particular, the most electorally successful parties and factions (outside the Kurdistan region) had begun a shift from sectarian agendas toward a center-ground of Iraqi nationalism in response to the popular demands unleashed by improved security. Today, those same parties are lurching back toward sectarianism under Iranian escort. Meanwhile, Iraqi popular demands for less divisive politics and more representative and effective government are being ignored.

And so, Iraq's future still hangs in the balance. The improvements in security and the new, democratic elements that have entered Iraqi politics make it possible to imagine Iraq slowly muddling upward, building gradually toward a better future. Iraq could someday emerge as a stable, prosperous, and even pluralistic society, one unlike any the Arab world has seen before. But, Iraq is not there yet, and it will take years, perhaps even decades, to realize that vision, even if the essential foundations are all there.

But Iraq could very easily slip down much worse paths. The Iraqis need to establish a government that can actually govern and that enjoys broad legitimacy among the country's different constituencies. Iraq remains a deeply dysfunctional society: its infrastructure, education, health, economy, sanitation and water networks, agriculture, and legal and industrial systems desperately need repair, redefinition, and institutional guidance. Similarly, a plethora of critical outstanding differences remain and could produce new rounds of violence. The hydrocarbon law, the status of Kirkuk and other disputed territories, as well as the relationship among the central government, the provinces, and the Kurdistan Regional Government are only the best known. All of these problems desperately need to be addressed, but are complex, long-term challenges that will require a mixture of patience, skill, luck, and outside support. Ultimately, they can only be addressed by a new Iraqi government, one with the political strength to strike compromises, build institutions, let contracts, hire and fire personnel, and make laws that previous governments have lacked. Without such a government, and without at least a roadmap for progress on key political disputes, at best Iraq will stagger along as the sick man of the Gulf, bullied by its neighbors, unable to defend itself (militarily, economically, or diplomatically), and used as a constant battleground for its neighbors' proxies—effectively a larger version of Lebanon today.

At worst, the failings of the government will allow and enable militias to reemerge, lay claim to territory and population, and wage civil war—like Lebanon at its worst in the 1980s or Bosnia in the 1990s.

Americans, policymakers and citizens alike, must realize the omnipresent potential for Iraq to slip into all-out civil war. There are dozens of scenarios—from military coups, to official misconduct, to the assassination of one or two key leaders—that could spark all-out violence. The conflict might look somewhat different than before, perhaps featuring Arab-Kurd conflict, greater intra-Shi'ah fighting, or various parts of the Iraqi security forces warring for control of the state. But it does not require much imagination to see how it could happen all over again.

Many Americans seem to believe that the changes wrought by the transformation of 2007–2009 are permanent and make it impossible for Iraq to return to internecine warfare, and therefore even a clumsy, hasty American withdrawal from the country would not be disastrous. Iraq might be left a weak, ugly place, they reason, but there are many weak, ugly countries in the world and a weak, ugly Iraq would not be a threat to American interests. This is a dangerously misguided notion. Iraq absolutely can slide into the kind of all-out civil war that would jeopardize American interests by threatening all of the other countries of the Persian Gulf region.

Indeed, if Iraq does not find a way to muddle slowly upward toward greater stability, prosperity, and pluralism, it is far more likely that it will slide quickly backward into the chaos of all-out civil war than that it would simply muddle downward toward an unpleasant, weak, but minimally stable state that need not concern the United States. Again, the dynamics and form of a renewed internal war might differ from the spiral of sectarian violence of the first round, and it might take some time for the positive developments in Iraq to unravel, but within months or just a few years, Iraq would likely find itself plummeting back into the maelstrom and pulling America's vital interests down with it.

The Need for a New American Strategy for Iraq

Washington has amply signaled its intention to withdraw U.S. military forces from the country, sooner rather than later—perhaps as early as December 31, 2011, the date set by the 2008 U.S.-Iraq Security Agreement (SA) for the complete withdrawal of all American troops (unless a new agreement is signed extending that deadline). What is not clear, however, is what the United States hopes to accomplish before its troops depart and its other resources attenuate, or how it plans to reach its goals. Washington has announced a strategy to exit, but it has not yet formulated an exit strategy that will secure and sustain its interests in Iraq and the region.

Although U.S. influence in Iraq remains substantial, it is less than what it has been in the past. It is diminishing as American troops leave Iraq, as American resources are diverted elsewhere, and as the Iraqis themselves regain the ability to secure their country and govern themselves. This makes it all the more imperative that the United States have a clear strategic concept that establishes clear goals and well-defined objectives that can be achieved with this reduced panoply of tools. An American strategy for exiting Iraq must also include a ruthless prioritization among those goals and objectives to ensure that the United States directs its residual influence toward securing first what is absolutely vital, and only then whatever else is possible. America needs to learn to pick and choose where it tries to exert influence, lest by trying to do too much it squanders what influence it has.

It is important also to recognize that other actors are still taking their cues from the way the United States operates in Iraq, not least many of the Iraqis themselves. If the Iraqis, the Iranians, the United Nations, and others see the United States headed for the exit with no discernible goal other than to leave behind a flimsy political structure as a façade, they will act accordingly. America's allies will make no effort to exert themselves in the event of a disorganized exit, and America's enemies will seek to capitalize on the fear such an exit will create. Specifically, the militias, the terrorists, and Iraqi citizens alike will all make decisions under the assumption that America's precipitate exit could lead rapidly to civil war. In that case, as has been the case in Iraq and countless other intercommunal civil wars over time, average Iraqis and their leaders will take actions to hedge their bets and save themselves, which will make that civil war inevitable. Thus, if Washington fails to develop a strategy to secure and sustain its interests in Iraq, it is likely to create the worst-case scenarios it should be seeking to prevent.

Given these constraints, it is essential that Iraqis see themselves as benefiting from continued American involvement in Iraq. The United States must be constantly on guard not to enflame Iraqi nationalism by acting in an overbearing fashion. American personnel cannot behave like the viceroys of Iraq and demand that Iraqis simply obey their orders. Iraqis bristle at outsiders meddling in their affairs, with a shorter fuse when it comes to the country which only recently held the legal status of an occupying power in their homeland. Americans now have to negotiate, cajole, wheedle, bargain, threaten (subtly), and use all of the other arts of persuasion. And the more the Iraqis believe that the relationship with the United States is of value to them, the more desirous they will be of preserving ties to the United States, and the more willing to overlook American interference or see it as positive, and the more afraid they will be of losing those ties.

AMERICAN GOALS FOR IRAQ MOVING FORWARD

It is critical to start by outlining American enduring interests in Iraq as a foundation upon which to build a framework for U.S. policy toward Iraq moving forward. It is impossible to develop a workable strategy without first defining clear goals. The Obama administration's decision to withdraw U.S. forces relatively quickly has changed American interests in Iraq in several important ways from those that prevailed as a result of the Bush administration's desire to try to stay for a longer period and draw down more slowly. Washington needs to explicitly acknowledge those shifts and then develop concrete plans accordingly.

Currently, the United States can reasonably claim to have several different goals as it exits Iraq. But these goals, and the objectives they imply, are not all of equal importance, and Washington must set clear priorities among them. Simply put, it may not be possible for the United States to achieve all of its goals and attain all of its objectives given the new situation and the reduced resources now available. Therefore, it is critical to understand what is of greatest importance and what is of lesser consequence when apportioning energy, attention, and remaining resources. Only by setting such priorities can the United States apportion its effort in what will inevitably be a complex and difficult disengagement process that aims to help Iraq keep moving forward.

The following should be the order of U.S. priorities in Iraq.

Iraq Cannot Be Allowed to Descend into Civil War

Iraq is an extremely important nation in one of the most economically vital and geo-strategically sensitive regions of the world. If it were to be consumed by a new civil war, this alone would have important consequences. However, the history of intercommunal wars like that which Iraq began to experience in 2005–2006 demonstrates that there is an inevitable tendency for such conflicts to spill over into neighboring states. At its worst, such spillover can cause civil wars in the neighboring states and/or trigger regional conflicts among the neighbors as they seek to protect their interests, secure resources in the carcass of the state in civil war, and prevent their rivals from doing the same.

Consequently, the absolute minimum that the United States must seek to achieve in Iraq is to prevent the outbreak of a new civil war. Unfortunately, this is no easy feat. Although it is clearly the case that the vast majority of the Iraqi people do not want to return to violence, comprehensive scholarship on the causes and drivers of civil war has demonstrated that popular opinion is largely irrelevant. What causes civil wars to occur and recur is the breakdown of the state's capacity to govern and secure its society, coupled with elites who believe that their goals are best served by resorting to violence. In Iraq today, the state's capacity to control Iraqi society has greatly improved since the summer of 2003—or even the dark days of 2006—but it remains fragile and uncertain. It is clear that a number of important Iraqi political leaders only agreed to stop using violence in favor of the political process because the events of 2007–2009 demonstrated that continuing to pursue a violent course of action would lead to their defeat at the hands of American military forces and American-backed Iraqi military forces. As in countless other intercommunal civil conflicts, there is every reason to fear that if those leaders feel that their aspirations are not being fulfilled through the political process *and* changed circumstances make them believe that a return to violence would pay greater dividends, they would take up arms again, regardless of what "the people" wanted.

It is in part for this reason that intercommunal civil wars have a dangerous tendency to recur. Extensive academic work on intercommunal civil wars akin to what Iraq experienced in 2005–2006 demonstrates that roughly half of the time a country falls back into civil war within five years of a cease-fire. Moreover, when the country in question possesses valuable natural resources, like diamonds, gold, or oil, the likelihood rises even higher.[2] Thus, Iraq is highly vulnerable to a resurgence of civil war, and the forces that could drag it back into conflict are omnipresent, floating just below the surface of Iraqi politics. Specifically, the militias and insurgents are down, but not out; fear and anger remains pervasive; and it is impossible to know how many Iraqi leaders still believe that they would be better off with a return to violence than a continuation of peace—or the conditions under which they might take up arms again.

If Iraq slips into all-out civil war, it will be disastrous for the security of the Gulf. As history has demonstrated, major intercommunal civil wars inevitably generate large-scale refugee flows, secessionist movements, terrorism, economic disruption, the radicalization of

neighboring populations, and foreign military interventions throughout the wider region. Indeed, Iraq in 2005–2007 was generating every
single one of these manifestations of spillover among its neighbors,
and examples of worse abound from Congo to Lebanon to Yugo-
slavia to Somalia to Afghanistan. In many cases, the spillover from a
major intercommunal civil war in one country can cause civil war in
another country, and/or spark a regional war over the carcass of that
state.[3] All of this would be devastating to the Persian Gulf region and
America's vital interests.

As disconcerting as the history of recurrent civil wars and their
impact on their neighbors may be, there is an important silver lin-
ing. What the academic literature also demonstrates is that when a
major, external great power is willing to serve as peacekeeper and
mediator in an intercommunal civil war, the likelihood of a recurrence
falls considerably.[4] This, of course, is the crucial role played by the
United States in Iraq today. The key is that the United States needs
to be able to continue to play that role for some time to come—until
Iraq is fully able to handle its own security and diplomacy—while
preserving the space for its economy and politics to continue to develop.

Iraq Cannot Reemerge as an Aggressive State

In the immediate term, and for the foreseeable future, the greatest
threat to U.S. interests would be a descent into all-out civil war in
Iraq. Without question, this must be the principal driver of American
strategy toward Iraq and should remain as such for many years to
come. However, even as the United States does everything it can to
prevent the reemergence of catastrophic internecine conflict, it also
must keep in mind its other interests in Iraq—even if they are longer
term and, for now, of secondary importance.

In particular, the United States also has to work to prevent the
reemergence of a strong, predatory Iraq. This stems from the para-
doxical problem that in working to build a stable, self-confident Iraq
that would not relapse into internal conflict, the United States also
cannot help build one that is so powerful and overbearing that it will

threaten its neighbors. Washington needs to remain wary of building another Iraqi Frankenstein's monster, as it did to some extent with Saddam himself in the 1980s.

Americans still disagree vehemently over whether the 2003 invasion was the right answer to the problem posed by Saddam Husayn's regime, but there is no question that his aggressive use of Iraq's military and pursuit of hegemonic dominance destabilized the region and posed a serious threat to American interests. Washington's efforts in the 1990s to contain Saddam—whether one believes them to have been succeeding or failing—reflected a major commitment of American power and a major, ongoing expenditure of American diplomatic capital that the United States can ill-afford to have to duplicate today.

A strong, aggressive Iraq would pose a serious threat to the critical oil-rich U.S. allies of the Gulf Cooperation Council (GCC). Just as it would be disastrous for American interests to allow Iraq to slide into all-out civil war because of the threat it would create to those allies, so too would it be disastrous to allow Iraq to reemerge as a rapacious, militaristic state little different from the one that the United States expended so much blood and treasure to topple in 2003, and to contain for a dozen years before then. Ultimately, if an important American grand strategic goal ought to be either to diminish its military role in the Persian Gulf over time or to refocus it against the potential threat of a nuclear Iran, a sine qua non of both would be ensuring that Iraq is not itself a source of instability in the region and that is just as true of an aggressive Iraq as it is of a fractured Iraq.

Iraq Should Ideally Be a Strong, Prosperous U.S. Ally

It would certainly be preferable if Iraq emerged as a friend and ally. Washington can never have too many friends, especially in the Middle East and among the major oil-producing states. Given how much the United States has sunk into Iraq since 2003, the best return on that investment would be not only averting the worst, but creating some positive gains.

While we should be careful not to create exaggerated expectations, it is reasonable to expect that a strong, pro-American, prosperous, and democratizing Iraq would have a salutary effect on the wider region. A dynamic Iraqi economy would undoubtedly create positive spill-over effects through trade and investment with other regional states, particularly Jordan and Turkey. It would probably take decades, but there is also reason to believe that a democratizing Iraq that is seen as reaping the benefits of peace, stability, and prosperity would serve as a model to inspire other neighboring populations—similar to the way that Japan served as an important model for South Korea, Taiwan, Indonesia, and other East Asian states. If Iraq became the first (large) Arab state to satisfy the political and economic desires of its people and if it had a strong relationship with the United States, this could help mollify Arab anger at the United States and possibly suggest to some that following Iraq's path (including its pro-U.S. alignment) would be beneficial to them as well.

In addition, a strong, democratizing Iraq would be most likely and most able to withstand Iranian efforts to dominate the region. More-over, the success and appeal of a democratizing, law-abiding Iraq would throw Iran's increasingly autocratic behavior into stark contrast.

Nevertheless, while it would be very much in America's interest to see Iraq emerge as a strong, prosperous, and democratic state allied with the United States, *this represents America's maximal interest in Iraq and should be seen as an aspirational goal rather than an irreducible necessity.* An Iraqi ally would be very beneficial to the United States, but it is not crucial to American vital interests. Simply put, America's most important interest, both for its own economic needs and as a global superpower interested in safeguarding worldwide stability, is the free flow of oil from the region. Either an Iraq ravaged by civil war or a new, aggressive Iraq would threaten the flow of oil from the region. Iraq as an American ally could help preserve that oil flow, but it is not necessary for Iraq to be an American ally for that oil flow to continue unimpeded. In addition, Iraq lies on the fault line of the Sunni-Shi'ah divide, raising its importance to regional stability still further. Stability in Iraq is therefore important in heading off potential conflict between predominantly Shi'i Iran and the Sunni Arab states of the Levant and the Arabian Peninsula.

Consequently, the United States should attempt to foster an Iraq that is a strong, prosperous U.S. ally, although nothing that the United States does to advance this goal should come at the expense of preventing civil war and preventing Iraq from becoming an aggressive state.

OBJECTIVES FOR AMERICAN POLICY IN IRAQ

The preceding summary of American interests in Iraq inevitably points to a subsequent hierarchy of subordinate (or contributory) objectives that the United States should seek to attain in Iraq to make it possible to secure those interests.

Iraq Must Be Stable

This is the flip side of civil war. Since the overriding American goal must be to avert civil war, Iraq has to be stable. This then begs the question, what is necessary for Iraq to be "stable"? Some of the key components of stability would include:

IRAQ'S POLITICAL SYSTEM MUST BE INCLUSIVE. No major religious, ethnic, regional, class, or other group can feel excluded from the political system on the basis of its identity—let alone threatened by the new government.

IRAQ'S POLITICAL SYSTEM MUST BE FUNCTIONAL. A dysfunctional political system could result in the breakdown of the state. As discussed later in this report, there are critical issues in Iraq's Constitution that are incompletely or inadequately addressed. A key conclusion is that the United States should prioritize efforts to work with Iraqis (and the UN) to develop a program to address a number of key sources of dysfunctionality in the Iraqi political system stemming from deficiencies in the Constitution.

IRAQ'S POLITICAL SYSTEM MUST BE EFFECTIVE. The government must be able to deliver good governance, allowing/aiding the economy to function, ensuring the provision of basic services to the Iraqi people, ensuring the rule of law, and protecting the citizenry from threats foreign and domestic.

As an important aside, there is a potential tension between the need for the Iraqi political system to be inclusive and the need for it to be effective. The United States should not mistakenly assume that the need for inclusivity translates into a requirement for every government to be equally inclusive or to devise a Lebanon-like apportionment of key positions—in which case the government is likely to be incapable of governing effectively.

IRAQ MUST REMAIN A DEMOCRACY. The requirement that the Iraqi political system and government remain inclusive, functional, and effective essentially translates into a requirement that Iraq must continue to democratize. This is not an idealistic position; it is a practical acknowledgment that no other system of government could realistically meet all of these criteria simultaneously.

THE IRAQI ECONOMY CANNOT "COLLAPSE." Severe economic problems could cause the breakdown of the state, creating the conditions for a slide into civil war. This is a different requirement from the need for the Iraqi political system to meet the obligations of the Iraqi economy listed earlier. That point relates to the government's ability to meet the needs of the citizenry, which if not done could indirectly lead to war by demonstrating the powerlessness of the government; this is about avoiding conditions that would lead directly to civil war by creating conditions of chaos.

THE IRAQI SECURITY FORCES CANNOT COLLAPSE. The Iraqi security forces are strong but not necessarily cohesive. As a result, severe political strain could cause them to fragment—which would produce chaos and the conditions for an immediate resort to civil war.

THE IRAQI SECURITY FORCES CANNOT BE HEAVILY POLITICIZED. Because of the fragility of the Iraqi Security Forces, there is a high likelihood that a coup d'état by an Iraqi military commander would fracture the military—with some segments opposing the coup makers out of professional, political, ethnic, religious, regional, or personality differences. Consequently, the United States should strenuously attempt to prevent a coup. By the same token, civilian efforts to politicize the military to keep it from launching a coup could either backfire and produce the coup that was meant to be prevented, or else could cause segments of the military to split from the political leadership because they saw a threat to their professionalism, corporate identity, or independence.

THE UNITED STATES MUST HELP IRAQ ACCOMPLISH ALL OF THESE OBJECTIVES. As noted, historically, the ability of an external great power to play the role of mediator and peacekeeper is extremely important in helping a state avoid the resurgence of internal conflict. In Iraq, that role is played by the United States. On their own, Iraqis have problems accomplishing any of the above-listed goals. With several notable exceptions, especially the Sadrists, Iraqi political leaders recognize the value of the U.S. role. The challenge, following the formation of a new Iraqi government, will be finding a mutually acceptable way for the United States to continue to play this role until it is no longer required. If requested by Iraqis, Washington should be prepared to retain a military presence in Iraq to buttress these functions.

THE UNITED STATES MUST PRESERVE ITS OWN INFLUENCE IN IRAQ. Because the United States needs to ensure that Iraq avoid civil war, and because that will probably require continued mediation and peacekeeping by an external great power (which is, again, the United States) it is therefore critical that the United States preserve its own ability to continue to play that role.

THE IRAQIS MUST SEE THEMSELVES BENEFITING FROM CONTINUED AMERICAN INVOLVEMENT IN IRAQ. The more the Iraqis believe that the relationship with the United States is of value to them, the more desirous they will be of preserving ties to the United States, and the more willing to overlook American interference or see it as positive, and the more afraid they will be of losing those ties (creating leverage for Washington).

THE UNITED STATES MUST BE CAREFUL NOT TO ENFLAME IRAQI NATIONALISM BY ACTING IN AN OVERBEARING FASHION. Iraqis are extremely nationalistic and bristle at any country meddling in their affairs. For some Iraqis, this is particularly true for the United States, which many Iraqis blame for the 2005–2006 fighting. There is an obvious tension between the United States' need to preserve its influence by taking a light touch when involving itself in Iraqi affairs, and its need to help the Iraqis overcome some of their problems— which could potentially require a much heavier hand.

THE UNITED STATES SHOULD WORK WITH ITS ALLIES AND INTERNATIONAL GROUPS AS MUCH AS POSSIBLE. Working closely with the United Nations Assistance Mission in Iraq (UNAMI) and other international organizations and countries simultaneously allows the United States to add their leverage to its own, and typically makes it far more palatable for Iraqi leaders to adopt foreign proposals.

Iraq Should Be Constrained in Its Ability to Wage Aggressive War, and Be Unlikely to Want to Do So

Operationalizing this objective is easier to accomplish in some ways, but harder in others, than stabilizing the country. Limiting Iraqi capabilities is fairly straightforward, if politically sensitive. The harder part is finding a way to channel Iraqi intentions. This is especially difficult since efforts to constrain Iraqi capabilities will probably never fully compensate for the military weakness of the GCC countries.

THE UNITED STATES SHOULD RETAIN ITS MILITARY PRESENCE IN THE REGION. As long as American forces are present in the region, it is unlikely that Iraq would attempt a conventional military attack on any U.S. allies.

The United States should try to retain an American military presence in Iraq both to reassure Iraq and hinder Iraqi aggression. It will be even harder for Iraq to go to war with another country against Washington's wishes if there are American military forces still in Iraq. Moreover, the presence of American military forces should also reassure Iraqis that they themselves are not threatened by their neighbors (particularly Turkey and Iran), none of whom would take action that would risk a clash with American military forces. Of course, it is critical to remember that Iraqis *must want* the United States to retain forces in their country.

THE UNITED STATES SHOULD TRY TO PRESERVE ITS ROLE AS IRAQ'S PRINCIPAL MILITARY PARTNER. Again, both as a deterrent to Iraqi action and a deterrent to threats against Iraq (which could tear apart delicate political progress or provoke Iraqi aggression in response), it is critical that the Iraqi armed forces be closely tied to the U.S. armed forces.

As its chief military partner, the United States should attempt to retain its role as Iraq's principal source of weaponry, training and support. Major arms sales (tanks, APCs/IFVs, artillery, multi-role fighter aircraft, helicopters, SAMs, warships) are the most visible symbol of the military-to-military partnership between the United States and Iraq. However, they serve two other critical purposes:

—Major arms sales make Iraq militarily dependent on the United States. Elsewhere, the United States has prevented its allies from taking aggressive military moves simply by refusing to provide logistical support for their intended operations. No other major arms supplier has done the same. Nothing could reassure Iraq's neighbors more that Baghdad would be prevented from attacking them than large-scale American arms sales. It is what GCC leaders are calling for in private.

—Having Iraqi military personnel train with Americans, attend American military schools and training programs, and rely on American military doctrine helps inculcate critical values of professionalism and abstention from the political process that could help avert a coup or other forms of politicization.

THE UNITED STATES SHOULD HELP IRAQ BECOME REINTEGRATED INTO THE REGION AND INTERNATIONAL COMMUNITY. In the U.S.-Iraqi Strategic Framework Agreement (SFA) there is already a long-term framework in place between Iraq and the United States to accomplish parts of this goal, while other aspects of this goal are contingent on the actions of the country's neighbors and the broader international community.

—*Helping Iraq restore its full international standing.* The United States should provide Iraq with diplomatic assistance to fully emerge from Chapter VII UN Security Council sanctions and settle its outstanding issues with Kuwait. This would be an important symbolic milestone and free Iraq to focus its diplomatic efforts on forward-looking issues rather than dealing with the legacy of Saddam Husayn's regime.

—*Promoting Iraq's reintegration into the international economic system.* In the SFA the United States has a tool to help direct Iraq's orientation outward to the international system through trade, investment, and cultural ties. Greater Iraqi integration into the global economy, including with the European Union and Asia, can only help to stabilize the country and provide economic growth opportunities that could help transform the zero-sum nature of Iraqi politics and regional ties.

—*Building a regional security framework that includes Iraq, the GCC states, the United States, and possibly other American regional allies (Turkey, Jordan).* If a new Iraq can be anchored in some kind of security architecture—an alliance system, a security organization like the OSCE, or at some point an arms control regime like CFE—it is far more likely that it will feel far more constrained in its ability to use force, less threatened by its neighbors, better able to deal with its security problems through diplomacy and (in part for the reasons just mentioned) more closely tied to the United States and its allies in the region. It will also likely make Iraq's neighbors much more comfortable with the emergence of a strong new Iraq, thereby reducing the problem of regional security dilemmas. A second parallel track would attempt to build a broader security organization for the region that includes Iraq, the United States, and the GCC, but potentially could someday also include Iran and other great powers as well. Such an organization would provide all of the states of the region the opportunity to discuss their security concerns and hopefully address them by non-violent means.

AMERICA'S ABILITY TO EFFECT CHANGE IN IRAQ

The preceding list may seem daunting, especially if one gives in to the inaccurate, but widely heard, impression that the United States has lost all influence in Iraq. Again, the end of the American legal status as occupying power, the drawdown of American troops, and the concomitant diminution of American resources devoted to Iraq has unquestionably diminished America's influence in the country. However, it is one thing to recognize this reality and something entirely different to extrapolate that the United States has no more (or only very little) influence left in Iraq.

In actuality, the United States remains extremely influential in Iraq and is likely to remain so for some time to come. What has changed has been the nature and sources of American influence. Influence no longer flows from the simple, overpowering sources it once did—a UN mandate, 160,000 troops, and tens of billions of reconstruction dollars. Today, it comes from dozens of subtler sources, which make it more difficult to see and wield. But these many wellsprings do combine into a very powerful stream.

For the United States, there is influence in leaving Iraq and influence in being willing to remain. Washington must learn to wield them both, deftly and often simultaneously. President Obama was not elected to keep U.S. forces in Iraq, and the Iraqis know it. That allows his administration to walk away from Iraq if the Iraqis won't do right by the United States. The United States must impress upon the Iraqis that whatever the United States is willing to continue to do for them comes in return for their willingness to continue moving in the right direction—toward greater stability, security, democracy, and respect for the rule of law.

It is not that President Obama is right and President Bush was wrong, or that President Bush was right and President Obama is wrong. Both administrations made important and fundamentally valid arguments about American interests related to Iraq, but both also overstated other aspects in support of their preferred policies. As usual, the truth lies in between, in a complicated intertwining of both sets of ideas. Given how complex and fragile the situation in Iraq has become, and given the other constraints on the United States' influence over that situation, Washington must learn to employ both the advantages of staying and those of leaving to give the United States the best chance to secure its interests on its way out.

Influence from the Ongoing American Military Role

In the military realm, the United States continues to provide the Iraqi Security Forces with critical support—combat enablers like air power, medevac, and real-time intelligence, but also the trainers, advisors, and even some partnered combat units that have proven so critical in building the competence, cohesion and professionalism of the Iraqi Army and police. Much of the leadership of the Iraqi Security Forces (ISF) continues to worry that a sudden withdrawal of American troops would lead to a rapid erosion of professionalism and effectiveness, and allow the reemergence of the same kind of corruption, sectarianism, nepotism, and divided loyalties that crippled the ISF in the past.

In addition, the American military presence as peacekeepers is important for Iraq's people and its leadership. The improvement in security brought about by the surge has allowed average Iraqis to feel safe enough to resume normal lives. Iraqis are increasingly confident in their police force and increasingly anxious to see American soldiers gone—but not yet. Today, they still like to know that the American soldiers are there in the background because it reassures them. Indeed, polls conducted at the time of the American troop drawdown in August 2010 found that 60 percent of Iraqis felt that it was not the right time for the United States to be withdrawing forces from the country.[5]

Furthermore, while the Iraqi Security Forces have made significant strides in combating internal threats to stability, senior Iraqi officials (including the minister of defense) have publicly stated that Iraq will need U.S. help in defending itself against external military threats after 2011. Key Iraqi concerns include their inability to defend their borders or to control their airspace in a heavily armed neighborhood with a history of wars. The chief of staff of the Iraqi armed forces, Gen. Babakir Zebari, has stated that Iraq will not be capable of defending its borders until 2020 and that if "America withdraws its forces and one of the neighboring countries causes problems, then we're going to have a problem."[6] Iraqis have no desire to trade a U.S. occupation for the possibility of unchecked incursions by neighbors, particularly Iran, who have little desire to see a strong, unified Iraq reemerge as a significant player in the region. The fact that Iraqis continue to regard U.S. military support as critical in guaranteeing Iraq's sovereignty against external threats is another crucial source of potential leverage for Washington.

The Strategic Framework Agreement

There are still literally hundreds of things that the United States is doing for Iraq. The United States still provides some critical economic and political assistance from capacity building in Iraq's federal and local government institutions, to micro-loans, to military equipment, to technical expertise. It is why so many Iraqi governors and mayors are despondent that they will be losing the American Provincial Reconstruction Teams.

Ultimately, the greatest source of American influence in Iraq moving forward is likely to be the provision of additional assistance in a vast range of different areas—from military operations and weapons sales, to capacity building, education, almost every aspect of economic reform, and a slew of major diplomatic matters. The foundation for this future cooperation is a little-known but critically important document known as the Strategic Framework Agreement (SFA), which the United States and Iraq signed in late 2008 at the same time that they also signed the Security Agreement (SA) governing the continued presence of American troops in Iraq until December 31, 2011.[7] It is important not to make too much of the SFA. It is nothing but a framework; an empty shell for the United States and Iraq to flesh out as they see fit over the years. There is little more than general exhortations regarding the broad types of aid that could be provided, without any specification of time, dates, quantities, or other details.

Nevertheless, whereas the SA tends to be controversial in Iraqi politics because it governs the presence of American troops, the SFA is much less so because Iraqis desire continued American aid, investment, and assistance in many areas of public life. In fact, it was the Iraqi government that proposed the SFA as a way of demonstrating that the bilateral relationship was no longer to be defined principally by security issues. The SFA also seeks U.S. diplomatic assistance in helping Iraq regain the international standing it had prior to Saddam Husayn's disastrous invasion of Kuwait in 1990. A great deal of American effort, both as a permanent member of the United Nations Security Council and through its close relationship with Kuwait, will be required to lift what Iraqis consider to be humiliating UN obligations and excessive reparation payments to Kuwait that date to the Saddam era.

Even Iraqis who would like to see every American soldier gone from the country often favor the aid and assistance encompassed by the SFA. Thus, the SFA and the potential for continuing American aid to Iraq across the board and well into the future is a powerful source of leverage for the United States. *At bottom, anything that the Iraqis want is a source of leverage for the United States*, especially if it is not something that the United States needs for its own, independent interests.

Because U.S. forces are leaving Iraq, American interests there have changed fundamentally. It is no longer the case that the United States *needs* to make an across-the-board effort to rebuild Iraq's economy, industry, agriculture, education, sewage system, electrical grid, road network, or the like. Rather, the United States has a direct interest in preventing the collapse of the Iraqi economy, but not necessarily in preventing Iraqis from living in needless poverty. The transformation of politics in Iraq has put the onus on Iraq's politicians, not the United States. When Iraqis complain about the poverty of their lives, they blame Baghdad, not Washington. Consequently, better governmental and economic performance is now something that the Iraqi leadership needs for its own interests—specifically, to maintain its legitimacy in the broadest sense, and for individual politicians to win and hold power in the narrowest sense. Progress on governance and economics has largely switched from being something that the United States needs the Iraqis to do for its interests, to being something that the Iraqis need help doing for their own interests. If U.S. resources, technical know-how, and encouragement of transparency and oversight mechanisms in government can help to make a dent in these problems, they can be an important demonstration to the Iraqi people of the benefits of continued U.S. involvement in Iraq and a source of leverage for America as its relationship with Iraq begins a new chapter.

Conditionality

Thus, there should be no question that the United States retains great influence in Iraq and could continue to do so for some time to come. The key is to know how to use that influence, and that tends to be the rub. As the preceding discussion illustrated, the most important source of American influence moving forward is conditionality. Virtually all American assistance needs to be conditioned on Iraqis doing the things necessary to achieve the objectives for American policy in Iraq outlined above, which in almost every case is likely to be something that is in the best long-term interests of the Iraqi people and the Iraqi nation, albeit not necessarily in the short-term interests of various Iraqi politicians.

That is going to be the key for American policy in Iraq moving forward: How to use the aid the United States is still willing to provide to convince Iraqi leaders to take the difficult decisions necessary to satisfy America's minimal requirements (avoiding civil war or the reemergence of an aggressive Iraq) and possibly even to achieve maximal U.S. aspirations (a prosperous, democratic, pro-American Iraq). It will mean conditioning specific aspects of American activities on specific, related aspects of Iraqi behavior. But it will also mean tying much wider aspects of American cooperation with Iraq, to progress in the Iraqi political system toward greater stability, inclusivity, and effectiveness. Ultimately, it means conditioning the continuation of the entire U.S.-Iraqi relationship on the willingness of the Iraqi political leadership to lead their country in this direction, which America, along with so many of the Iraqi people, want to see it go.

CHAPTER TWO

POLITICS

Politics has become the center of gravity of the American effort toward Iraq. But we don't mean American politics. We mean that the future of Iraq will be principally determined by the course of its domestic politics, and that in turn will determine whether America's vital interests there are safeguarded. Security in Iraq has improved significantly, but it will only hold over the long term if Iraqi politics sorts itself out and is able to provide for the people, govern the country, and resolve its internal antagonisms. If Iraq's domestic political framework collapses, so too will the country's security. Iraq's economy continues to sputter along and it will only improve when there is a government in Baghdad able to govern effectively, harness Iraq's oil wealth, and use the proceeds to redevelop the entire country. Moreover, if there is going to be an economic collapse in Iraq, it will almost certainly come from some failure of Iraq's domestic politics (like mismanaging the oil sector). In other words, while a civil war might technically be the result of a deterioration in the security situation or an economic meltdown, in actuality the many things that could give rise to such situations now lie largely, if not entirely, in the realm of politics.

The United States and Iraqi Domestic Politics

Because Iraq's domestic politics is the key to the future stability or instability of the country, and because it remains so fraught, it must be the principal American focus as the United States extricates itself from its outsized involvement in Iraq. Failures in Iraqi domestic politics are the surest route to threatening America's vital interests in Iraq because they carry with them the spark of civil war. Consequently, the absolute highest priority for the United States during the ongoing drawdown and for the next several years must be to see Iraq's domestic politics work out right. That means continued respect for democracy, transparency, and the rule of law; continued development of bureaucratic capacity; no coups d'état; no dictators; reconciliation among the various ethno-sectarian groupings, as well as within them; a reasonable delineation of center-periphery relations including a workable agreement over the nature of federalism; and an equitable management and distribution of Iraq's oil wealth, as well as the overall economic prosperity that must result from such distribution.

The problem is that domestic politics may well prove to be the one area where Iraq's political leadership will stop at nothing to keep the United States out. Iraq's political leaders have a less than stellar record of playing by the rules of democracy and enforcing the rule of law. Especially when they are in positions of authority, there has been a dangerous tendency to skirt, avoid, or flat-out ignore the Constitution in both letter and spirit. Iraq's political leadership tends to be dominated by former warlords, clerics, tribal shaykhs, and expatriates, few of whom have experience with democratic processes and even fewer of whom seem to understand that respect for the Constitution establishes precedents and norms that will constrain their rivals just as it constrains their own behavior—and that that may someday be very important to them. Most struggle to find ways to play Iraqi politics the old-fashioned way and only grudgingly obey the rules when they must.

Since 2003, the United States has provided the ultimate insurance that no group will be able to completely overturn the system and dominate others. This is a U.S. role that many Iraqis continue to regard as at least a necessary evil if not a positive good. Most Iraqis want greater democratization, even if they don't always use the word. They want to see their new political system succeed and their leaders forced to deliver goods and services for them, rather than vice versa, which has too often been the case in Iraq. They want more transparency and more accountability and blame corruption for the dismal state of service delivery in the country. They want governmental institutions they can rely on and political parties that represent their interests rather than someone else's. They want all of the things that the United States wants.

Iraq's leaders recognize this as well and they fear the residual influence of the United States will force them to deliver. It is why those out of power regularly call on the United States to "play a more active role" in Iraqi politics, and why those in power often chafe at American interference in Iraqi politics. It is why Iraqi leaders in power call on the United States to stand aside and allow the Iraqis to solve their own problems, especially when those leaders are acting in an extra-constitutional or even entirely unconstitutional fashion.

Thus, it is important for both the future of Iraq and for America's vital interests that the United States focus its energy and resources on Iraq's domestic politics. Yet, domestic politics is also the arena in which Iraq's political leaders, particularly those in power, will be most determined to exclude the United States. For that reason, the United States must be prepared to subordinate virtually every other aspect of its Iraq policy by making major sacrifices in areas previously held sacrosanct, to maximize its ability to influence Iraq's domestic politics. It is why virtually every other element of the U.S.-Iraq relationship needs to be seen as leverage to get the Iraqis to do the necessary in the one area of greatest importance to us (and to their own long-term best interests as well). For this reason, the political arena should be the one where America applies conditionality most clinically.

As important as Iraq's domestic politics is to American interests, it is critical that the United States recognize its own limitations. The United States can shape Iraqi politics—and wields far more influence than many Americans seem to recognize—but shape is all it can do. The United States cannot dictate to the Iraqis anymore. Especially between 2003 and 2006, Americans often drew up virtual blueprints for the Iraqis and then demanded that they adopt the U.S. project in toto. Those days are gone. In fact, much of the success that the United States enjoyed in 2007–2010 has been a result of new American political and military leaders who recognized this reality and were far more solicitous of Iraqi views. It is that practice that must continue and even expand in the face of the diminishing American role in Iraq and the reemergence of Iraqi sovereignty and nationalism.

Indeed, attempting to dictate to the Iraqis would badly backfire on the United States. Iraqis remain deeply nationalistic, and any sense that the United States is interfering in Iraqi affairs will engender a quick and powerful backlash from the Iraqi public. Those Iraqi leaders who see their interests threatened, either by the specific positions being pushed by the United States or by a more general sense that the Americans will not allow them to act the way they would like (typically because of U.S. constraints and checks on the group in power), will be able to use heavy-handed American behavior against the United States. If it happens too often, it could undermine the ability of the United States to influence Iraq's domestic politics altogether. In addition, Washington needs to recognize that it is competing for influence in Baghdad—particularly with Tehran, but also to a lesser extent with Riyadh, Damascus, and a number of other regional governments—and overbearing American behavior can cost the United States in that contest.

For that same reason, *the United States must work in tandem with UNAMI, other international organizations, and its allies (in the region, Europe, and elsewhere) more than ever before.* The acceptance of the UN as a well-meaning and neutral arbiter continues to grow among Iraqis. The more that the United States can move in synch with the UN, or better still, allow UNAMI to take the lead and simply support them behind the scenes, the more palatable and influential American initiatives will be. Similarly, Britain, Japan, Turkey, Jordan, and the UAE have all played a constructive role in Iraq in recent years and the United States would do well to partner with them more frequently—perhaps even turning appropriate gambits over to them altogether. Some of Iraq's most important neighbors, particularly Saudi Arabia and Iran, have more often been problems, rather than solutions to problems in Iraq, but the United States should continue to work on the Saudis in hope of brokering a more constructive Saudi-Iraqi relationship in the near future.

A Partnership, Not a Suicide Pact

Saying that the United States has vital national interests invested in the future of Iraq's domestic politics is not the same thing as saying that the United States should remain committed to Iraq under any and all circumstances. Quite the opposite.

The United States needs the Iraqi leadership and the Iraqi government to take certain actions and behave in a certain fashion. The United States should use its residual influence to move Iraq's leaders in that direction and should reward their cooperation generously for doing so. Indeed, as long as the Iraqi leaders are moving their country in the direction that serves American interests—the direction of greater democracy, rule of law, transparency, accountability, non-violence, and communal reconciliation—the United States can and should remain willing to help the Iraqis generously.

However, the United States must acknowledge that the Iraqis may choose not to move in that direction. As noted, many Iraqi leaders resist the rule of law, constitutional limits, and other constraints as irritating and unnecessary. They would very much like to ignore them if they could and, especially when they are in position to do so, they may regard America's role in Iraq as a hindrance to their acting as they please. Similarly, Iraqi leaders have often refused to take positions in public that they believe necessary to Iraq's future welfare but are unpopular in the short term. In particular, Iraqi politicians have been unwilling to support a continuing military relationship with the United States—even if they privately believe it to be necessary for Iraq's stability—because they fear taking a position that could be portrayed as a betrayal of Iraqi nationalism. In addition, at least some Iraqi politicians fear that Tehran would do much worse than simply campaign against them if they publicly advocated pro-American positions that the Iranian government regards as anathema.

Consequently, there is no guarantee that the Iraqis will do what the United States needs them to do, even though it is manifestly in the best interests of the Iraqi people that they do so. If that proves to be the case, the United States needs to be prepared to scale back or even end its commitments to Iraq altogether. Of course, not every little thing the Iraqi leadership does need be a make-or-break decision. There will doubtless continue to be cases in which Iraqi leaders will make bad decisions but the United States will opt to tough it out with an eye on the longer term. But the exceptions cannot become the rule. And the United States will need to regularly make clear which issues rise to such a level of criticality regarding Iraq's future stability that U.S. relations with Iraq could shift significantly if Baghdad acts recklessly.

This is a crucial aspect of how America's ongoing involvement with Iraq must be conditional on the Iraqi leadership keeping up its end of the bargain. If Iraq's leaders are not willing or able to act in a manner consistent with good governance, the rule of law, and the need for national reconciliation, then the risks to Iraq's future stability are so grave that they should cause the U.S. government to reevaluate the level of its commitment to the U.S.-Iraqi partnership and the resources it is willing to invest in it.

THE SOURCES OF POTENTIAL POLITICAL COLLAPSE

Despite the significant progress of the past seven years, and particularly since the surge in 2007, Iraq nevertheless is still a fragile state.

Governance remains weak and in many cases personalized, primarily as a result of a lack of effective institution building since the fall of Saddam Husayn's regime in 2003. The focus of the Iraqi political parties that were brought to power since then has been primarily on consolidating and protecting their new political, economic, and security prerogatives at the expense of their rivals.

As such, the state institutions that have evolved have been weak and characterized by political factionalism. Appointments to ministries and other state institutions, especially in the economic and social services spheres, have been driven primarily by the notion of "sharing the pie" of power and patronage, rather than by qualification or competence. Ministries themselves have therefore become political fiefdoms and massive graft machines in many ways, with jobs and services allegedly provided at times on the basis of ethnic, sectarian, or party affiliation—a problem that was particularly manifest during the worst days of the sectarian conflict. In the process, politicization of the ranks of the civil service has accelerated, which has diminished technocratic competence, especially as experienced personnel have been culled, either as a result of age or perceived links to the former regime. Thus, the institutional vacuum created by the U.S.-led invasion and collapse of the Iraqi state has never fully been filled, and Baghdad has struggled to extend its power and administration throughout the provinces, much to the chagrin of residents and local governments in many areas.

Complicating these problems have been two core issues that have remained unresolved and that threaten stability and the functioning of the Iraqi government: the dispute over federalism and the absence of progress toward genuine national reconciliation. While Iraq is defined as a federal state in the 2005 Constitution, serious disagreements remain over the extent to which decentralization is mandated, and ultimately over where sovereignty lies. This issue does not just divide Arabs from Kurds (and Irbil from Baghdad), as is commonly assumed. There has been a lack of common vision among Iraq's various Arab constituencies. Some Islamist Shi'i parties, such as the Islamic Supreme

Council of Iraq (ISCI), have promoted a sectarian-based system of regions, modeled on the power of the Kurdistan Regional Government. ISCI has since backed away significantly from these ideas, but some officials in individual provinces, notably al-Basrah (and to a lesser extent Maysan and al-Anbar), have more recently sought extensive decentralization of power for themselves, with some of the same security and economic authority—including over hydrocarbon resources and revenue—that Irbil has amassed. On the other side of the equation, a majority of Iraqi Arabs—Sunni and Shi'i—appear to favor preserving Baghdad's centralized authority; they see Kurdish efforts and tentative similar moves by Shi'i groups as serious threats to the territorial integrity of Iraq.

This festering dispute has undermined both governance and stability, and should therefore be a critical focus for U.S. policy moving forward. Until now, the failure to reconcile the rival visions of federalism has been papered over through ambiguity—as in the case of the Constitution, subsequent legislation on devolution of power, and the budget. This has blocked the passage of key laws altogether, including the hydrocarbon and revenue sharing legislation. Worse still, Irbil and Baghdad have pursued policies based on their own interpretation of their constitutional mandates, widening the gap between them and complicating the steps that will need to be taken to accommodate their rival visions of the state, not least because of the growing mutual mistrust between the two sides. For the Kurds, creating what amounts to a confederacy of Kurdish, Sunni, and Shi'i regions *throughout all of Iraq* is viewed as an existential priority to ensure that no future government in Baghdad will ever have the power to repeat historical abuses and past ethnic cleansing against Kurds. But each initiative Irbil takes to facilitate this objective—and to block the central government's efforts to restore its former power—raises the hackles of Arab politicians in Baghdad who suspect that the Kurds' ultimate goal is the dismemberment of Iraq. The Kurds in turn interpret what they see as foot-dragging on fully implementing decentralization provisions called for in the Constitution as evidence that the mind-set in

Baghdad has not really changed. These mutual concerns and fears have driven political leaders there to ever-more hard-line reactions, raising the risk of local confrontations escalating out of control while holding up key national events such as elections and the census.

The absence of progress toward genuine national reconciliation is similarly destabilizing. While Iraq has embraced representative politics to a considerable degree, Iraq's new leadership has refused to clarify unambiguously who can participate in government and under what terms. In fact, it has often allowed the most radical groups and individuals to manage this process and establish the framework for determining who is in and who is out. Thus, de-Ba'athification procedures have been abused for political benefit, especially among Islamist Shi'i politicians seeking to protect the gains they have made since 2003. Both the process and the institutions that administer it lack full legislative underpinnings, and the refusal to draw a line under the procedures—or to institute a truth and reconciliation process comparable to post-apartheid South Africa's—create political disruptions (as was evident in the runup to and after the March 7, 2010 election). In the longer term, this will be a ticking time bomb if Sunni and nationalist constituencies feel that de-Ba'athification is being implemented as a way of denying them a legitimate share of power.

Left unaddressed, the disputes over federalism and national reconciliation could unravel the progress toward stability. At the very least, they will retard Iraq's ability to become an effective, well-managed state, dooming it instead to continued muddling-through and ineffective governance. As such, resolving the disputes should be a priority for Washington. Tensions between Baghdad and Irbil, and between the KRG and neighboring Iraqi provinces, have been high for some time, with occasional threats of violence. Indeed, U.S. military commanders still talk of it as the most vulnerable fault line in Iraq. But Baghdad could also face unmanaged challenges from elsewhere in the country, as recent regionalism initiatives in al-Basrah attest.[1] Meanwhile, ambiguity over political participation rights could spark violent antipathy among constituencies formerly associated with the insurgency in the west and north-west of Iraq. Many of these groups remain deeply suspicious of the new regime in Baghdad, and the Islamist Shi'ah that dominate it, suspecting that they will never create the space for other constituencies to share political power. For them, the specter of periodic purges and exclusion from power under the guise of de-Ba'athification will limit the extent to which genuine national reconciliation is possible.

Addressing these issues will be a difficult task. It will require considerable time and attention during a period when American public interest in and support for involvement in Iraq is clearly waning; it will necessitate a level of nuanced understanding of Iraqi political dynamics that has often proved beyond the capabilities of U.S. policymakers in the past; and it will involve occasionally taking a tough line with groups that have hitherto benefited from being close allies of the United States. But the costs of not facing up to these challenges and adapting policy accordingly will be far greater.

Moreover, now may be an opportune moment for the United States to make this shift. The fog of post-election machinations in Iraq has partially obscured the fact that polls and the elections themselves have demonstrated a significant evolution of Iraqi politics over the past seven-and-a-half years. While sectarian and particularly ethnic fault lines remain clearly evident, the election illustrated new political trends that potentially provide Washington with the foundations to push these policy goals. The vote reinforced a growing sense that nationalist agendas enjoy broader support among Iraq's Arab constituencies (Sunni, Shi'i, and everything in between) than do crude sectarian ones, a factor that benefited Prime Minister Maliki's State of Law and Ayad Allawi's Iraqiyya coalitions in particular. Moreover, despite the prevalence of large electoral blocs based on common sectarian identity, Iraqi politics is now far more atomized than before, with a host of smaller parties, factions, and individual personalities competing on the basis of agenda politics, *even within the blocs*. Finally, there was a clear anti-incumbency sentiment, with a sense that Iraqis had lost some patience with the many of the established parties that were elevated to power by the United States in 2003, and were seeking alternatives offering different agendas and solutions to the problems of governance and violence that have dogged the country since then.

THE IMPORTANCE OF CONSTITUTIONAL REFORM

Over the past two years, as the United States has slowly stepped back from Iraqi politics, economics, and security, it has allowed Iraqi institutions to step forward and assume those responsibilities. In doing so, this process has revealed both the immaturity and incapacity of many of these institutions, as well as salient flaws that remain in the overarching system itself.

The United States cannot possibly hope to transform every Iraqi ministry or agency before it sheds its outsized role in Iraq over the next several years. Nor is it necessary for the preservation of American interests to do so. Yet, there are some key organizations that must be tended to. The security services/ministries are the most obvious (and are treated at length in the next chapter). So too are certain economic entities, particularly those governing water and oil (a topic discussed in the fourth chapter). These bureaucracies are absolutely critical to Iraqi stability, and therefore *American* interests in Iraq. Thus they must have a reasonably sound capability to deal with the problems in their sectors before the United States further reduces its commitments in Iraq. Most of Iraq's other institutions are of great importance to Iraq, but are not a priority for American interests.

Working with Iraqis (and the UN) to address flaws in the Iraqi Constitution, however, is absolutely critical to American interests in Iraq. The Constitution governs the interaction among all of the different institutions, establishes their authorities and prerogatives, and defines the relationship between the government and the governed. The shortcomings of the Constitution will have a profound impact on the political future of the country. Indeed, there is plentiful evidence that the Iraqis already find themselves caught on these

issues—from the disputes over the powers of the Iraqi prime ministership, to the endless wrangling over government formation following the 2010 election, to the daunting splits between the KRG and
the central government.

*The United States cannot be confident that its paramount objec-
tives of preventing civil war/instability in Iraq have been fully secured
until the Iraqis have appropriately addressed the remaining problems
in the Iraqi Constitution because they threaten the viability of the
state.* It would be fundamentally irresponsible for the United States
to assume that the Iraqis will be able to overcome the gaps in the
Constitution to achieve a stable polity without outside support. The
evidence available speaks to their inability to do so. Whenever the
Iraqis have hit political walls because of constitutional inadequacies,
the result has been deadlock, not cooperative efforts to find solutions
to the problem.

In some cases, there are many possible ways to address a problem
in the Constitution that would all be consistent with democratic principles and the unique circumstances of Iraq. In other cases, there may
be only one or two ways to deal with a flaw in the Constitution that
would not create other problems. What matters for the United States
is that the Iraqis make the changes necessary, in a way that is consistent with the Constitution's own terms, so that the Iraqi Constitution
is able to serve as an adequate foundation for a stable Iraqi state.

Gaps and Seams

The 2005 Iraqi Constitution is a remarkable document that represents the myriad of contradictions of a fragmented polity emerging
from totalitarian dictatorship and seeking to achieve a national compact on how to share power and resources. The Constitution establishes an electoral democracy (however imperfect), greater separation
of powers between the executive, legislature, and judiciary than Iraq
had previously known, and a bill of rights that serves as an important guide for creating a uniquely Iraqi form of a pluralistic society.
In a country with a history of concentrated power in Baghdad, the

Constitution has remade Iraq into a federal state by recognizing and providing genuine autonomy to the Kurdistan region and enabling the beginnings of administrative decentralization in the rest of the country. Since its adoption, the Constitution has increasingly become the reference point for Iraqi politics, with Iraqi politicians of all persuasions brandishing constitutional arguments to make their case on issues from government formation to oil contracting.

At the same time, the Constitution has not fully succeeded as a social compact in terms of important issues related to governance, state structure, and political reconciliation. Many of the document's shortcomings can be traced to its rushed drafting process. A number of factors combined to create a Constitution that embodied the deeply unsettled state of affairs in Iraq in 2005 rather than a sustainable compact. On the political side, these included the Sunni boycott of the political process, strikingly short drafting timelines, overrepresentation of political actors with a highly decentralized vision for the Iraqi state, and a prioritization of achieving short-term benchmarks over long-term thinking. In addition, the document is riddled with technical and procedural inconsistencies. In several instances the new charter papered over deep divisions on its most critical elements, therefore allowing it to be interpreted in different—and contradictory—ways by various players going forward. It seems unlikely that Iraqi politics and institutions can continue to evolve toward stability post-2010 when there are serious cracks in the underlying foundation.

Iraq's Constitution does not adequately address many of the issues that today hamper political reconciliation and the consolidation of democratic governance in the country. This is something that the Iraqis themselves recognize. In late 2008, the Iraqi Parliament, the Council of Representatives (CoR), issued a statement stressing the need for all Iraqi authorities to work together on constitutional amendments to guarantee the stability and unity of the country as well as the principles of its federal democratic system.[2] It is vital to Iraq's future stability that these gaps be addressed through a crucial set of political understandings to enable the passage of constitutionally mandated laws or even constitutional amendments to fill out governance structures and political frameworks.

The priorities that the United States must focus its efforts upon and help the Iraqis address include:

POWER AND RESOURCES. Agreeing on the distribution of power, oil revenues, and territory between the federal government in Baghdad and Iraq's only existing autonomous region (Kurdistan).

STATUS OF KURDISTAN. Clarifying whether arrangements between the Kurdistan region and Baghdad should be the inspiration for Iraq's overall federal system (as is currently the case) or a constitutionally guaranteed exception to it in light of the Kurds' unique history and governing capacity.

NEW LEGISLATION. Crafting constitutional amendments and legislation that will establish a key set of legislative and judicial mechanisms that in most federations would be responsible for resolving possible center-periphery conflicts, including:

—More nuanced principles for resolving disputes between regional and national law (currently the Kurdistan region, future regions, and possibly even ordinary provinces can simply override national law on most matters, including perhaps those related to oil and revenue sharing);

—Creating an upper house of Parliament;

—Forming inter-governmental commissions and independent institutions; and

—Enabling easy, regular interaction between federal and regional judiciaries.

CHECKS AND BALANCES. Creating checks and balances in Iraq's executive branch to diminish the dominating role that the prime minister has been able to acquire in practice and share power more equitably among the president, prime minister, and the Council of Ministers (the cabinet).

POST-ELECTION PROCESS. Properly defining the process of forming a government after parliamentary elections.

Iraq's Constitution must not only define the structure of the Iraqi state and order its government and laws, but also serve as a national compact on the sharing of power and resources among its diverse communities. This was always recognized by Iraqis and Americans alike as one of its most critical purposes. In this sense, the Constitution is a "peace treaty," a vehicle for inter-communal reconciliation to overcome the toxic legacies of both Saddam Husayn's totalitarianism and Iraq's post-2003 civil strife. The issues identified above go straight to the heart of questions related to the shape of Iraq, perceptions of its viability and territorial integrity, and fears about what the overconcentration of power either geographically in Baghdad, or personally in terms of a leader, might result in at some point in the future. The Constitution at best currently offers an incomplete guide to resolving these issues and it is difficult to foresee how Iraq can make decisive political progress without a strategy for addressing these gaps.

Process

Constitutions are by their nature intended to protect core political and governance structures (and the compromises often necessary to define those structures) against change by transient political majorities. Iraq's Constitution is no different. It is protected against amendment by special procedures and super-majority requirements. Efforts from 2006 to 2008 to review the Constitution ultimately foundered on the Kurdistan region's effective veto over the process. Likewise, the implementation of a Political Reform Document that opponents of Prime Minister Maliki attached to the SA in November 2008 came to nothing as a result of the extended electoral competition cycle that began with the January 2009 provincial elections, ran through the March 2010 parliamentary elections, and continued into the protracted negotiations over government formation that followed.

The sequence, process, and timing of constitutional reform are therefore likely to be of great significance. In contrast to the quick-fix approach of 2005, the United States must view its support of an Iraqi constitutional review effort as a long-term endeavor. Unresolved constitutional issues must be first identified and addressed by political negotiations among the key players, and only then resolved by a set of complementary amendments to the Constitution that can ultimately be put to the Iraqi electorate as a single national compact. It is difficult to envision a more piecemeal approach to constitutional amendments working. Iraq's main power brokers have consistently adopted a "nothing is agreed until everything is agreed" mentality. Moreover, foundational issues cannot be addressed without the broad support of all political parties and groups. *A single, all-embracing proposal of amendments that allows the scope for trade-offs between various Iraqi groups appears to have the best chance of creating the basis for the Constitution to be accepted as a national charter.* But it is likely that this will only emerge (if at all) as a result of a patient multi-year effort. What is now required is basic agreement on the outlines of a roadmap for getting there.

U.S. support for constitutional reform should therefore focus on working with Iraqi leaders post-government formation to help them identify the problems and contradictions extant within the Constitution that are impeding political and security progress; separate those that can be fixed through legislation from those that will require constitutional amendment; and develop a consensus on a long-term vision for enshrining political accommodations into a comprehensive package of constitutional reform.[3]

Federalism

The issue of federalism in Iraq is often mistakenly confined to Arab-Kurdish issues, when it in fact also encompasses schisms among the Shi'i Arab community as well as fears among Sunni Arabs about their future political and economic place in Iraq. There are two basic questions Iraqis must eventually answer to arrive at a consensus on what type of federalism is appropriate for their country. The first is the distribution of power and territory between the federal government in

Baghdad and Iraq's only existing autonomous region of Kurdistan. The second is whether these arrangements should serve as the model for the relationship between Baghdad and possible, future federal units. Both of these issues are fundamentally related to the shape of Iraq, perceptions about its viability and territorial integrity, and fears about what actions an overly strong central government in Baghdad might take at some point in the future. Given the overriding importance of oil revenues to the Iraqi state, they also directly relate to the extent of Irbil's control over Kurdish oil fields, the disposition of the bountiful oil of mainly-Shi'i southern Iraq, and the relative paucity of oil in Sunni areas.

The current tensions surrounding Arab-Kurdish struggles over territory have overshadowed the fact that the greatest point of controversy in the constitutional drafting process was not the autonomy of the Kurdistan region. This was generally (albeit sometimes grudgingly) accepted following the de facto separation of Kurdish areas from the rest of Iraq after the Gulf War in 1990–1991. Rather, the most significant disagreement concerned the formation of new federal regions outside of Iraqi Kurdistan, particularly if they were to have the ability to span multiple provinces and amalgamate sectarian communities. It was the Constitution's promotion of this possibility that caused Sunni Arabs and other Iraqi nationalists, including some prominent Shi'i clerics, to view federalism as a codeword for partition. And it was the prospect of multiple federal regions that would have complete autonomy over their own affairs while also controlling Iraq's vast southern oil reserves which led some constitutional experts to question the viability of Iraq's new state and national government.[4]

In many ways these highly decentralized arrangements are a forceful response to the excessive centralization of power under the Ba'ath Party and how this power was wielded to commit mass murder against the Shi'ah and Kurds. In addition, the Constitution either ignored or only minimally addressed a key set of institutions and procedures that in most federations are typically responsible for coordinating competing priorities and resolving center-periphery conflicts. These include the establishment of an upper house of Parliament, inter-governmental advisory bodies and commissions, and the procedures for basic inter-operability between federal and regional judicial systems, as well as the setting of core capacity requirements (sufficient to prevent a collapse in governance) that any proposed new federal region would have to demonstrate before it could assume that status. Most critically, Article 115 of the Constitution established a very simple, even crude mechanism whereby regions can override national law on most matters, including possibly those related to oil and revenue sharing. Given the criticality of oil to the Iraqi state and the geographic concentration of Iraq's most valuable oil reserves (and its only ports) in Maysan and al-Basrah governorates, the potential exists for there to be a gaping geographic and economic hole in the heart of the new Iraq should either province ever elect to become a region either singly or jointly.

If anything, since the adoption of the Constitution, Arab-Kurd positions on federalism have hardened along with the rise of tensions between Baghdad and Irbil over disputed territories and oil contracting authorities. In contrast, Sunni and Shi'i positions on the formation of new regions appear to have converged as the sectarian conflict abated from 2007 onward. Shi'i views on federalism have always been complex, but parties like the ISCI, which in 2005 advocated for the formation of a super-Shi'i region in southern Iraq, appear to have lost ground to movements seeking to position themselves as Iraqi nationalists, like Nuri al-Maliki's State of Law and the Sadrist trend. ISCI's own support for federalism also appears to have mellowed after the strong performance of Iraqi nationalists in the January 2009 provincial elections. The United States might usefully explore the willingness of Iraqi actors to explicitly separate the issue of a Baghdad-KRG accommodation from the shape of federal arrangements for the remainder of Iraq—a concept that has come to be known as "asymmetric federalism."

Asymmetric federalism would seek to preserve the Kurdistan region's current status, but as a constitutionally guaranteed exception to Iraq's overall federal system rather than the inspiration for it. From this starting point, it may be possible to make progress toward rethinking the shape of federal arrangements outside of the Kurdistan region as well as to bank amendments on important coordinating institutions mentioned above. (The KRG has an interest in ensuring its voice is heard in Baghdad through regional representation in an upper house of Parliament and the formation of inter-governmental coordinating bodies.) In contrast, the core elements of a power-sharing agreement on security, political, and oil matters between Baghdad and Irbil likely need to be separately addressed as part of comprehensive Arab-Kurdish talks that include the status of Kirkuk and other disputed territories.

Oil-for-Soil

There are no easy solutions to the related conundrum of Iraq's disputed internal boundaries. The parties involved have been in unrelenting pursuit of zero-sum-game solutions in which one ethnic group's territorial gain constitutes another group's loss, despite promises of minority rights (which, when offered by one side, are distrusted by the other). The various tracks designed to yield a solution have instead all led to dead ends, most importantly the process under Article 140 of the Constitution. This being the case, the United States and UNAMI should encourage the Iraqis to consider a different approach to the problem.

Rather than addressing the issue piecemeal, it might be worth taking a comprehensive approach in pursuit of a package deal that incorporates related unresolved concerns such as control and management of oil, the sharing of revenues, and the division of power between the federal government and the Kurdistan region. The final deal would have to take into account the principal stakeholders' core requirements without crossing their red lines. Such a deal would then have to be reflected in a package of constitutional amendments under Article 142 of the Constitution.

The Kurds would have to accept Kirkuk's special status as a stand-alone governorate neither under Baghdad's direct control nor Irbil's. This would be for an interim period and include a mechanism for resolving Kirkuk's status at the end of this period. In exchange, the Kurdistan region would obtain demarcation and security guarantees for its internal boundary with the rest of Iraq and have the right to manage and profit from its own hydrocarbon wealth through licensing and exports.

The federal government would also have to accept such a special status for Kirkuk, as well as special rights for the Kurdistan region with respect to hydrocarbons management. In exchange, the federal government would set national standards for oil and gas contracts and give the Kurds access to Iraq's hydrocarbon export infrastructure. In addition, Article 115 (and similar articles) of the Constitution would have to be revised to refer to only the Kurdistan region in order to create an asymmetric system of federalism.

Revenues would continue to be divided between Baghdad and Irbil based on an agreed-upon percentage for the Kurdistan region, following a population census. As for disputed districts in other governorates, areas that have significant majorities of Kurds should be joined to the Kurdistan region, starting with areas that are already administratively part of one of the three Kurdish governorates. The rest would stay linked to Baghdad as they are today, with security provisions and power-sharing arrangements designed to protect all minorities living in these districts.

Negotiations toward such a package deal should start as soon as a new government is formed. As a first confidence-building step, the new Council of Representatives could start working on a revenue-sharing law. Meanwhile, the United Nations Assistance Mission in Iraq should revive the High-Level Task Force and start talks toward resolving the low-hanging fruit, i.e., the districts with significant Kurdish majorities. It should also foster support of local communities in the disputed territories for an eventual deal by carrying out confidence-building steps based on UNAMI's April 2009 report and encouraging broad participation.

Executive Power Sharing

From the start, those deciding on the nature of the executive branch in the Iraqi Constitution were intent on keeping it weak. The prime minister was to be more of a manager than a political powerhouse. The Council of Ministers, i.e., the cabinet, was to govern together with the prime minister in a form of collective executive under strong legislative oversight.[5] Under the Constitution, the presidency was meant to be a largely ceremonial post, although the president has the right to propose legislation and presidential concurrence is required on key decisions by the prime minister, such as a declaration of a state of war or emergency, or a recommendation to dissolve Parliament and hold new elections. More recently, the perception that Prime Minister Nuri al-Maliki has sought to build an independent power base around the office of the prime minister, his success in creating extra-constitutional structures, and his ability to at times avoid apparent constitutional restrictions, has panicked many of his rivals. They fear that he, or his successor, may use the powers of the prime ministership to make themselves a new dictator. This has put the issue of the concentration of executive power at the forefront of Iraqi politics, paralyzing virtually all other government activity.

The problem is not a straightforward one. Maliki and his supporters contend, not without considerable evidence, that the inefficiencies of the Iraqi system and the gaps in the Iraqi Constitution require a strong prime minister willing to take the initiative to force the system to act if the government is to do anything at all. Indeed, as we noted above, one of the problems with the Iraqi government so far, and one that must be addressed if Iraq is to emerge as a stable state, is its inability to govern effectively. Weakening the executive could exacerbate this problem. Consequently, the key must be to find a way to create checks and balances on the prime minister without weakening the executive overall.

The Constitution's delineation of executive authorities is brief. It describes the prime minister as the "direct executive authority" of the state, commander-in-chief of the armed forces, and chair of the Council of Ministers. The president is designated as the "symbol of unity" and "guarantor" of commitment to the Constitution. For the first term of the Iraqi government only (2006-2010), the president was replaced by a temporary three-person Presidency Council that had an explicit veto power over legislation passed by the Iraqi Parliament. The temporary Presidency Council, as well as the Constitution's parallel requirement of two deputy prime ministers for the first term, also served to informally ensure representation of Iraq's three major ethno-sectarian groups in each part of the Iraqi executive.

The separation of powers within Iraq's executive authority has been a key issue of dispute in the constitutional review process. The Sunni community, fearful of untrammeled power being wielded by a Shi'i majority and hopeful one day of holding the presidency, put forward a parcel of proposals aimed at increasing the power of the presidency and strengthening the Council of Ministers (CoM). These focused on temporarily transferring the commander-in-chief function from the prime minister to the president in times of war or emergency and providing the president a role in the appointment of senior military officers. These proposals were resisted based on the (Shi'i) counterargument that they would move Iraq toward a presidential rather than parliamentary system, and if this were to occur, the president should be directly elected. The 2010 government-formation process has served as a catalyst for exploring the use of various tools to create a more balanced executive, including by keeping the multiple deputy premier and vice president posts, strengthening the role of the Council of Ministers, and enhancing the president's authorities.

Iraqis in fact have several options for clarifying the existing executive power-sharing framework, including informal political understandings, laws, and constitutional amendments.[6] Possible steps for refining executive power, which could be taken without constitutional amendments, include:

—Giving the president the right by law to ask the Federal Supreme Court to rule on the constitutionality of any legislative bill or proposed action by the prime minister or CoM.[7] (The president already has the power to submit a request to Parliament to withdraw confidence from the prime minister.)

—Fulfilling the Constitution's existing requirement for passing a law to organize the work of the CoM, which has not fully realized its constitutional responsibility of being a deliberative body for executive decisionmaking. (Under the Constitution, the CoM has the authority to plan and execute state policy, including the budget, as well as propose laws, maintain oversight of ministries and the National Intelligence Service, and nominate the appointment of senior civilian officials and military officers to Parliament.)

—Codifying in legislation the role of a Political Council for National Security, with the power to review security and financial issues, if such a body emerges as a part of political agreements leading to government formation.

—Codifying in legislation the roles and mission of the minister of defense as well as other key senior leaders in the armed forces. And, clarifying the primacy of the minister of interior relative to internal security measures except in times of declared extremis.

While relatively easy to achieve because they do not require constitutional amendments, for the same reason, the above measures might prove inadequate to the task. Laws can be repealed by a new constitutional majority, and so far, the mechanisms created by the Constitution for judicial review have had little impact on the prime minister's prerogatives. Even in these circumstances, however, any such political agreements and associated legislation could help create a body of precedent to fill out constitutional gaps. The core principles undergirding these understandings could possibly later receive constitutional enshrinement along with any agreed-upon changes to the executive structure that cannot be accomplished without direct constitutional amendments.

Given the potential inadequacy of these measures to address the fundamental problems raised by the ambiguous delineation of executive authorities, it may well be necessary to pursue constitutional amendments. Such amendments should seek not to disperse executive authority, but to create checks and balances, in particular by strengthening the president to serve as a counterweight to the prime minister, and possibly dividing the areas of governmental activity between them. Specifically, such amendments could include:

—Shifting the function of commander-in-chief of the armed forces from the prime minister to the president, with CoR confirmation of all ministers of defense and security, as well as the intelligence and military chiefs. This would give the president lead responsibility on national security affairs and provide a critical check on the authority of the prime minister.

—Extending the Presidency Council and its legislative veto authority, or simply granting the president a legislative veto.

—Providing for the direct election of the president. This would enhance the president's position, and might be necessary if the powers of the presidency were to be expanded.

Government Formation Procedures

Iraq's two post-Constitution governmental formation exercises have been protracted, messy affairs. While they have to some extent forced power sharing, the downside has been the vacuums created by the extended government-formation periods. These periods have brought substantial risk to the political and security situations in both 2006 and 2010. They have also effectively paralyzed long-term government policy and decisionmaking for significant periods of time. These experiences suggest clear constitutional rules and procedures on contentious issues, such as government formation. This is as important to coherent and representative Iraqi decisionmaking as is the institutional separation of powers.

Iraq's Constitution actually has relatively detailed timelines and responsibilities for government formation (in contrast to other countries' constitutions). It sets a sequence of deadlines for the first session of Parliament (fifteen days after the certification of election results), election of a new president by Parliament (within thirty days of the first session of the CoR), nomination of the prime minister (by the new president within fifteen days of election), and presentation of the prime minister's government and program to Parliament for its endorsement (within a further thirty days). The new president is given the direct responsibility to charge "the nominee of the largest Council of Representatives bloc" with the formation of the government. In 2006, the largest electoral coalition was divided over its nominee and took months to settle the question. In 2010, Iraqis were unable to agree as to whether the largest bloc requirement referred to the electoral coalition that won the most seats in the election or the post-election coalition that secured the most seats. The chief justice of the Federal Supreme Court did not help matters by offering an opinion that the Constitution was consistent with both interpretations. In 2005 and again in 2010, Iraqis took substantial time to work through these issues and got around constitutional timeline requirements through "pausing" the government formation clock by holding the first session of Parliament open indefinitely.

To some extent, difficulties in government formation are therefore more an artifact of Iraq's (extreme) proportional representation electoral system—which makes it highly unlikely that any single party will win a majority in Parliament—than directly attributable to government formation procedures themselves. The electoral system almost guarantees that Iraq will have coalition governments. Combined with the divided nature of Iraqi society, this generates extensive post-election politicking and requires agreement on an entire range of positions (who will be president, prime minister, speaker of Parliament, key ministers, etc.) before a government can be formed.[8]

Constitutional clarification on two issues could help ameliorate (but given the nature of Iraqi politics not eliminate) the threat of similar delays in future electoral cycles. The Constitution needs to more precisely define the term "largest Council of Representatives bloc" so that it is clear which entity has the first crack at post-election alliance building and government formation.[9] Because of the inherent drawbacks of a pure proportional representation system in a fragmented polity like Iraq's, this would likely mean that the formal grouping that wins the most votes in the election (not the largest post-election coalition) would have the first opportunity to form a government, and if it failed, the group that got the next largest number of votes in the election would have the next chance to do so.

In addition, as is the case in other countries, the Constitution could set out the consequence of new elections if a government is not formed within a defined period of time. In order to avoid a deadlock in the process (as Iraq experienced in 2010), the date for calling new elections could be a certain number of days from the certification of electoral results rather than from the first session of Parliament (for example 120 days, which would correspond to at least two prime minister nominees having the opportunity to propose a government if the constitutional timeline was strictly followed). The Constitution could also diminish the amount of time available to a candidate in which to present a government after getting the chance to do so. This might allow three or even four candidates to attempt to form a government before the requirement for new elections. Iraqis have often commented upon their inability to reach difficult consensus unless faced with a hard and fast deadline, and the repercussions of a constitutional requirement for a new election could provide this discipline in the future.

CHAPTER THREE

SECURITY

At present, all American troops are scheduled to depart Iraq by December 31, 2011, when the current Security Agreement between Iraq and the United States expires. Nevertheless, there are clear potential security and political benefits of a continued American military presence in Iraq after that date if it is agreed to and requested by the Iraqis. Both the United States and Iraq have compelling national interests in establishing and sustaining a long-term relationship across the political, economic, and security realms. In the near term, a continued presence of U.S. troops is likely to help sustain Iraq's recent security gains and provide some insurance and confidence that basic rules of the political system will be respected. The forces required in future would likely be modest—less than what the United States now maintains in Germany, Japan, or South Korea. The strategic effect of their presence, however, could be enormous.

Yet, it is not the case that maintaining an American military presence in Iraq is so compelling that it should override all other considerations. This is clearly a topic of great sensitivity to Iraqis, as well as a subject within U.S. domestic politics. Iraqis desire a relationship with the United States that is not limited to the security sphere, and as has been frequently cited, have strong nationalist tendencies that translate into resentment of external influence in their affairs and foreign troops on their soil. At the same time, while most Iraqis are eager to see the U.S. forces leave, they are anxious as to how the resulting vacuum will be filled. Many, especially those not directly in power, do not yet fully trust their security and political institutions. It is therefore possible for a continuing U.S. troop presence to be broadly accepted, but only if it is perceived as being requested by Iraqis, negotiated in a transparent manner between the U.S. and Iraqi governments, and approved by Iraq's Parliament.

Moreover, from the U.S. perspective, retaining American troops in Iraq makes sense only if those troops have sufficient authority and capability to secure American interests in Iraq's continued stability. Thus conditionality must also govern even the key question of whether the United States maintains a continuing military presence in Iraq. The odds of such a mutually beneficial outcome being achieved will be improved by the extent to which the U.S. and Iraqi governments are able to demonstrate clear benefits to the Iraqi population resulting from the Strategic Framework Agreement in the non-security realm.

ROLES AND MISSIONS

U.S. forces in Iraq today have already moved into a supporting role behind the Iraqi Security Forces (ISF), and they are no longer leading combat operations. The critical tasks for which they are needed now and after December 2011 instead fall into five broad categories:

—Conducting peacekeeping and confidence-building measures, particularly along the Arab-Kurd border;

—Supporting U.S. and international civilian operations;

—Supporting ISF development, including the slow separation of the Iraqi Army from internal security affairs and the transition to police primacy;

—Guaranteeing Iraq's sovereignty against external military threat; and

—Conducting residual counterterrorism operations, together with the ISF, against al-Qa'ida and affiliated Sunni terrorists, as well as against violent Shi'i groups supported by Iran.

All of these missions will continue to be important, and sound American and Iraqi policy would support a U.S. posture that could fulfill all of them. However, President Obama's decision to draw down U.S. military forces and other resources committed to Iraq faster than the timetable required by the SA will inevitably require prioritizing among these missions. In some areas, the United States will have to accept a lesser level of effort and a greater level of risk. However, prioritization should not be taken as a justification for failing to adequately resource all of the military requirements.

Bolstering Internal Stability

Flowing from the preeminent American interest in preventing an internal crisis that could trigger a civil war in Iraq, by far the most important mission is to support Iraq's internal stability. The sectarian war in Iraq has ended, and new conflicts (between Arabs and Kurds, various Shi'i groups, or the Sunni and the Shi'ah) have been averted—so far. But because states torn by civil war are prone to relapse, particularly in the absence of external forces, it is critical that this set of missions be the United States' highest priority.

PEACEKEEPING. American troops continue to play a critical role as peacekeepers in Iraq. This is true both generally for the country writ large, and for several important specific cases.

Most Iraqis, even those who dislike the American military presence, tend to regard it as a necessary evil.[1] Used correctly, U.S. troops are potentially a crucial substitute for the trust that undergirds stable societies. Trust will also be a critical element in allowing a shift from the Iraqi Army to national and local police responsibility for internal security. But, rebuilding trust in Iraq, as in all societies broken by intercommunal conflict, will take years, and in the meantime, the Iraqis need some powerful external force to reassure them that their rivals (including rivals in the government) will not be able to use force against them. Realistically, that external force can only be American.

There are a variety of important, smoldering conflicts that American troops have shown themselves able to police, thereby ensuring that they have not ignited and consumed the entire country. There are still tens of thousands of "Sons of Iraq" (SOIs)—former Sunni insurgents—who switched sides as part of the *Sahwa*, the "Awakening" movement. The SOIs have become an important bellwether for the Sunni community, demonstrating the willingness of the Shi'i-dominated government to reconcile with Iraq's tribal Sunnis. American forces continue to serve as liaison, guardians, and even something like parole officers for many of the SOI groups who have not yet been integrated into Iraq's sputtering economy, who fear the government, and who have at times fallen prey to both terrorist attack and government mistreatment. These groups still trust the American military to defend their interests, and it is unclear what their fears might drive them to do absent the U.S. presence.

Similarly, despite American hopes for asymmetric federalism and an "oil-for-soil" compromise between Baghdad and Irbil, it seems unlikely that the Arab-Kurd dispute will be settled anytime soon. The leaders in Irbil and Baghdad all remain deeply suspicious of one another, and over the past two years, at places like Khanaqin and Mosul Dam, small reckless moves have nearly led to wider conflict. Such skirmishes along the so-called "trigger line"—a line of control separating Kurdish Peshmerga forces from federal army forces—could escalate into wider battles, endangering Iraq's stability and potentially expanding to include Turkey and even Iran.

American forces along the trigger line significantly reduce the likelihood both of bad decisionmaking in Irbil or Baghdad and of the escalation of local security incidents into major conflicts. Former U.S. Forces-Iraq Commander General Ray Odierno established a series of tripartite security checkpoints along the trigger line, combining American, ISF, and Peshmerga forces. He also established procedures and mechanisms for clear communication between the ISF and the

Peshmerga, and between Irbil and Baghdad, via American forces that both sides accept as honest brokers. These Combined Security Mechanisms (CSMs) have dramatically reduced the likelihood of incidents along the boundary and have even more dramatically reduced the chances that any incident will escalate. American forces have been improving the ability of both the ISF and the Peshmerga to patrol the disputed areas and they ensure transparency that allows both sides to understand each other's movements and intentions.

The presence of American forces in Iraq can also reduce the likelihood of more deliberate aggressive behavior by the Kurdistan Regional Government or Baghdad. Kurdish leaders have repeatedly made clear their desire for real, direct guarantees of their security from the United States, which from their perspective should include weapons sales, training for the Kurdish Peshmerga, formal statements by American officials, and an expanded, long-term American military presence in the KRG. They see such a partnership with the U.S. military as a strong deterrent against Arab adventurism and therefore the foundation of their own long-term well-being and prosperity. Both the Bush and Obama administrations have been wise to refrain from promising the Kurds too much in these areas, both because any such arrangements would have to be agreed to by the national government, and because doing so could also encourage the Kurds to overreach in their negotiations with Baghdad. Consequently, any such arrangements on security for the KRG need to be part of an American package of incentives to the Kurds and should only be provided as part of either an all-encompassing "grand bargain" or a series of interlinked deals between Irbil and Baghdad that resolve all of their key differences.

As important as the peacekeeping mission is, it can probably be performed by fewer American forces over time. The more that Iraqi civilians and military forces interact with one another without conflict, the more that trust will reemerge among them. As we have seen in Sinai, Bosnia, Kosovo, and elsewhere, peacekeeping duties initially performed by powerful military formations can give way to smaller "tripwire" forces, which can eventually be replaced by small numbers of observers, and at some point ultimately eliminated altogether. For instance, the CSMs currently employ platoon-sized units of Americans working with equal-sized formations of Iraqi security and Peshmerga. Over time, the American platoons could probably be replaced by squads or even observer and liaison teams of four to six personnel.

There are several critical, related points to be made about further reducing American military manpower levels. Peacekeeping is largely a "presence" mission. It is best to *prevent* outbreaks of fighting than to have to step in and end them. Reducing military manpower inevitably attenuates presence because in many instances, there simply are not enough troops to be everywhere they are needed. This places a premium on intelligence gathering, both by those troops left in place and other available assets. It also means retaining adequate headquarters assets to ensure communications and preparatory, preventative, and cooperative actions among the peacekeeping forces. To prevent a firefight, the United States has to know about it, and know about it with enough time to get some kind of a force there to douse any spark before it can catch fire or spread. This too will require an adequate headquarters structure, meaning the right size and number of headquarters, to include support arrangements. Because the government itself is inevitably controlled by partisans of one side or another in post-conflict situations like Iraq's, it is also critical that this intelligence gathering network *not* rely on the goodwill of the host government for its information. Finally, because the United States will no longer have the military forces available to have a presence everywhere that might be needed, it will have to rely much more on quick-reaction forces (QRFs) held in reserve and able to deploy rapidly to any trouble spot. Likewise, the smaller groups of American troops who will be out advising Iraqi formations, securing convoys, and otherwise observing and monitoring will be inherently more vulnerable than larger, more heavily-armed formations—and they will need to be able to call on a QRF if they ever get into trouble—and will again need to be able to call on a higher-level headquarters structure to ensure that the QRF gets to them in time.

Improving Iraqi Civil-Military Relations. In 1932, Iraq celebrated its independence from the British Empire. Barely four years later, it experienced the first military coup d'état in the modern history of the Arab world. It has been all downhill from there. Iraq was the most coup-prone country in the Arab world prior to the Ba'ath Party's seizure of power (with help from elements in the Iraqi military they later purged). Even while Saddam ruled Iraq, he faced numerous coup threats, including from within his military and security services, and succeeded in quashing them only by constructing a Stalinist totalitarian state that comprehensively politicized the Iraqi military. In other words, the Iraqi military has a very long and sordid history of taking power, contributing to truly miserable civil-military relations.

Moreover, the history of Third World militaries conducting counterinsurgency campaigns is equally discomforting. Counterinsurgency is an inherently politicizing mission because it is an inherently political operation; as countless experts have opined in recent years, insurgencies are triggered by failures of the political system and they are only eliminated when the underlying grievances of the people supporting the insurgency are addressed. Not surprisingly, Third World militaries that have been trained to perform counterinsurgency campaigns, like that which the Iraqi security forces have waged since 2006, have an alarming propensity to overthrow their governments when foreign combat forces are not present to prevent this from happening.[2]

As long as American military forces remain in Iraq in strength, it is unlikely that the Iraqi military, or any of its constituent elements, would attempt to take over the government. Many Iraqi military officers want desperately to be disinterested military professionals and want nothing to do with politics, so long as the politicians do not try to politicize the military the way that Saddam did. But there are certainly other Iraqi officers who see the military as the only strong, unified, progressive institution in Iraqi society, and that perspective has been the starting point of many coups in the Arab world generally, and in Iraq specifically. It is the partnership with the United

States armed forces, which exerts enormous influence on Iraqi military thinking, that has prevented any Iraqi military involvement in politics. The culture of professionalism and apolitical deference to civilian authority is heavily ingrained in American military personnel and it rubs off on their Iraqi counterparts as long as the Americans are there. Unfortunately, many Iraqi political leaders, particularly the Shi'ah, remain wary of the security and intelligence forces because of their role under Saddam, and they have attempted to politicize them—if only to ensure that they follow their orders. Once again, it is the United States military that has been the primary impediment to this practice. The United States has pressured the government to remove incompetent, but politically connected officers and has blocked efforts by the political leadership to replace competent officers with more politically reliable ones.

The ISF's dependence on American support will continue to diminish, but it will not vanish any time soon. The variable in question is whether or not the United States will have military units in Iraq capable of serving as a deterrent. The bar here is low, but not negligible. An Office of Security Cooperation with a handful of mentors and trainers is insufficient. Such a presence has not deterred military coups in many states. Of those that have boasted a substantial American military presence, only a handful (principally Vietnam, South Korea, the Philippines, and Panama) have experienced military coups, and these occurred only with American connivance or disinterest. The stationing of American military units in Iraq will not be a guarantee against military challenges to the political order, but it will be a strong disincentive and thus potentially an important contribution to lasting stability.

Perhaps the greatest danger from an Iraqi military coup is that it probably would not succeed. The Iraqi armed forces have come a long way and are far more capable than they were even a few years ago. However, the military remains politically fragile and lacks cohesion. If placed under the enormous psychological strain of trying to seize power, the ISF would likely fragment along ethno-sectarian, tribal, regional, and even political lines. Moreover, regardless of which officer took power and why, other ethnic, religious, tribal, and political groups would inevitably see him as a partisan threat and would mobilize their supporters—including their supporters within the army—against him. In turn, he would attempt to rally his own ethnic, religious, tribal, and political comrades to his side. Thus, any attempted coup would likely fail and in so doing would cause the collapse of the armed forces and the outbreak of intercommunal civil war. Here as well, the U.S. military presence is crucial to averting a civil war, and therefore must be a priority for the Obama administration even as it seeks to draw down the American commitment to Iraq.

The American military presence has been equally important in persuading nervous Iraqis of all ethnicities and sects that they need not fear the ISF—a fear that has been rising as the United States has begun to draw down its forces in Iraq.[3] U.S. partnership was vital to encouraging Iraq's Sunni Arabs to accept an ISF working for a Shi'i government. It has also been essential to dispelling recurring fears and rumors of Sunni attempts to hijack the ISF and use it as a coup force to undo the effects of the 2003 invasion. It has been equally important in persuading the Kurds that a professional ISF is not an existential threat to Kurdistan. In each case, the persuasion has required more than mentors. Sunni, Shi'ah, and Kurds have allowed their fears to be calmed (to the extent they have been) because they believe that American military units present in Iraq would resist and, in some cases, prevent the ISF from undertaking sectarian cleansing, launching a coup, or starting an ethnic civil war. The logistical dependence of the ISF on direct American support has also played an important part in this persuasion.

Supporting American and International Civilian Operations

As much as security has improved, Iraq remains a dangerous place. There are still groups deliberately targeting Americans and other international personnel. There are still parts of the country where even the locals do not welcome outsiders. Nevertheless, American civilians and those from various international organizations, particularly UNAMI, need to move about freely to accomplish their critical tasks. Many of these personnel rely on American support and vehicles to get around the country. Because these personnel and their activities are critical to all of the various U.S. interests in Iraq, it is equally important that American military forces continue to provide for their security to enable them to do their jobs.

At the moment, the Obama administration plans to shift many of these responsibilities from the U.S. military to the State Department. This is a politically appealing but practically untenable course of action. The truth is that the State Department is unlikely to be able to perform a great many of these tasks because State is not well-equipped (literally and figuratively) to do so, and because State approaches such situations in the opposite manner from the military. It is not quite true that the State Department has not provided for its own security in high-risk environments. In places like Colombia, the State Department oversaw the use of Blackhawk helicopters and Humvees. But this is never a good solution. The State Department is not a combat organization and it must rely on security contractors to handle high-threat environments like Iraq, which has led to numerous problems in Iraq and elsewhere. The Marine guards that protect every U.S. embassy lack the numbers, the vehicles, the weapons, and the authority to provide protection to large numbers of American and international civilians working in Iraq's cities and countryside. Only American combat troops properly equipped and with the full authorization of the U.S. government will be able and permitted to fulfill that role.

In addition, for the military, casualties are a normal and expected element of completing a mission, whereas for the State Department, casualties constitute mission failure. There has already been an alarming decline in both the extent of American contact with Iraqis and the American civilian presence outside the embassy compound as the U.S. military has transferred its security responsibilities to the State Department. This practice needs to be reversed, not just slowed, and the only way that that will happen is to prolong the presence of U.S. military forces in Iraq, even if at levels well below their current strength.

Consequently, "transferring" many of these responsibilities to the State Department is likely to mean that they are simply not performed, not through any fault of State's, but because these kinds of tasks are not what the State Department was created or resourced to accomplish. The State Department is going to have tremendous difficulty providing the kind of security for a large American and international civilian presence that is needed to allow those civilians to continue to provide the kind of assistance that Iraq will want and the U.S. will likely wish to provide. The State Department is unlikely to be able to provide the kind of assistance to the Iraqi police force that will make both Washington and Baghdad confident that it will be able to handle a reliable transition to police primacy. The State Department certainly will not be able to play any kind of "peacekeeping" role should one prove necessary—and given the number of recent incidents between KRG and ISF units that American troops have defused along the trigger line, there is a high likelihood that someone will have to continue to play that role well into the future. Realistically, these missions can only be handled by the U.S. military.

Providing U.S. Military Support to the ISF

American military presence and assistance also provides important benefits to the Iraqi political leadership. It allows the Iraqis to focus resources on rebuilding their country rather than defending it, and enables the ISF to develop into an efficient, modern force operating at a level that would otherwise be unattainable. American advantages in intelligence collection, analysis, and dissemination, as well as in precision targeting, give the Iraqi leaders the ability to combat internal threats with much greater effectiveness and with much less collateral damage and civilian loss of life than their own forces could provide. American logistical support and technical advice allow the ISF to sustain advanced weapons systems that would otherwise be beyond their reach and give them potential operational mobility within Iraq that their own air forces could not provide. American air power, finally, is the main tool Iraq's leaders have with which to defend their airspace and maintain their air sovereignty.

Some of these benefits serve Iraqi interests more directly than they serve American interests. Consequently, it would be easy for Washington to fall prey to an overly narrow prioritization of American military missions that might see U.S. support to the ISF as being of secondary importance to the United States because it does not *directly* serve American interests, particularly the paramount interest of preserving Iraqi stability. Indeed, some might actually see it as counterproductive to the interest of preventing Iraq from emerging as an aggressive, expansionist state. But this misses a key point: support to the ISF plays a critical indirect role in promoting America's vital interests because it is a key to American leverage/influence over the Iraqi government and its political leadership more broadly.

American requests or pressure to make difficult choices will almost certainly be met with the question from Iraqi leaders, what's in it for us? If the answer is that the United States is offering only the kind of political, economic, and advisory assistance that directly serves American leaders, but not those of Iraq's own leadership, then the Iraqis are unlikely to alter their behavior on security matters to suit American desires. Effective partnerships require an exchange of benefits.

Thus, the United States cannot consider only those military missions that directly support the promotion of America's primary goals, like peacekeeping. *The United States must also recognize that its continued support of the ISF—by providing combat enablers, training, equipment, and even bureaucratic assistance—is a vital source of influence within the Iraqi political process.* At the very least, the United States should use these missions to continue to prevent excessive Iraqi governmental interference (i.e., politicization) of the military, as well as military involvement in politics or in settling political disputes, by making the provision of this assistance conditional on both sides' adherence to proper civil-military relations.

However, as a general point, continuing to provide such assistance will doubtless help preserve American influence in Iraqi politics in a wide range of ways.

ASSISTING THE DEVELOPMENT OF THE IRAQI SECURITY FORCES. U.S. support for the overall development of the ISF will not only create more political influence in Iraq, it will help secure U.S. interests on the ground. Since 2005, U.S. interest in the ISF has focused on creating Iraqi forces capable of taking over missions performed by American military units, thereby allowing U.S. combat forces to withdraw. That objective has largely been accomplished—U.S. forces have been reduced to 50,000 and withdrawn from major combat operations without any significant increase in violence thus far. Because the ISF has come so far, and is now much more capable than it once was, the United States can have relatively less concern about its ability to play its assigned role in maintaining the stability of the country.

Nevertheless, the ISF is not yet a fully functional military and police force, and until it is, Washington cannot have complete faith that it is in a position to prevent a civil war. If the ISF proves unable to maintain the gains of the last three years against al-Qa'ida, other Sunni insurgent groups, and Iranian-directed Shi'i armed groups, then American, regional, and global security will once again be put at risk. The capability of the ISF to do so with current levels of U.S. military assistance, let alone lower levels, remains unclear. The ISF has shown an ability to respond to enemy attacks well, defeating some, and deterring or disrupting others. It has developed significantly, but is not yet fully developed. In particular, it has not yet demonstrated the ability to conduct independent offensive operations against reestablished insurgent or terrorist sanctuaries within Iraq. Such operations in the past have almost always been led by American forces (with the notable exceptions of Basra and Sadr City, where there was nevertheless substantial American and allied assistance) because they are the most difficult military tasks in a counter-insurgency campaign.

There is no evidence one way or the other about the current ISF's capabilities to conduct such operations without American military support. U.S. Special Forces and other assets have continued to target al-Qa'ida and other Sunni resistance groups aggressively, and the ISF does not yet have the ability to take over those missions. The political paralysis following this year's elections has led to a significant reduction in ISF operations against Shi'i groups, many of which are linked to political parties that are vying for power and positions of influence in the new government. It is very likely that some of those groups have reestablished sanctuaries in key locations in Iraq's Shi'ah areas. The capability of those groups is unclear, as is their intent. They have largely refrained from large-scale violence during the period of government formation, but it is by no means clear that they will continue to do so.

Protecting Iraq from Regional Threats

On January 1, 2012—the date set for the withdrawal of all American troops—Iraq's military forces will be unable to defend the country's land or maritime borders or control and protect Iraq's airspace. That fact poses two dangers to America's interests in preventing the emergence of an aggressive Iraq and desiring Iraq to retain a pro-American alignment. It may encourage Iraq's neighbors to take advantage of Iraq's weakness, and it may encourage Iraqi leaders to try to build their own military forces to a level that is itself destabilizing. Both Iraq and its neighbors have historical reason to be concerned.

Iraq has been at war with its neighbors, the international community, and itself for over fifty years. Even before Saddam Husayn's congenitally aggressive approach to foreign policy, Iraq had been an enthusiastic participant in several of the Arab-Israeli wars, threatened Kuwait with invasion, nearly come to blows with Turkey and Syria over water and the Kurds, and generally been a net liability for regional security.

Of course, Iraq's neighbors have not been passive either and their actions continue to anger and frighten Iraqis. Turkey has regularly sent military forces into Iraq to hunt Turkish Kurds or punish Iraqi

Kurds. Syria, Turkey, and Iran manipulate the flow of water to Iraq in ways that imperil Iraqi agriculture, energy production, and even oil exports. Saudi Arabia and Syria have looked the other way when Salafi terrorists have crossed their territory to get to Iraq. In addition to the decades of past strife (including the horrific Iran-Iraq war), even while American military forces have been present in great numbers in Iraq, the Iranian military has violated Iraqi sovereignty on a number of occasions, shelling Iraqi Kurdistan, seizing oil wells on Iraqi territory, and overflying Iraqi airspace.

In all of these post-Saddam cases, the Iraqi response so far has been moderate and muted. The presence of American troops and aircraft in Iraq has undoubtedly contributed greatly to this moderation—Iraqi leaders preoccupied with internal problems have been confident that U.S. forces would not permit any large-scale or protracted foreign adventurism in their territory and so have not felt a need to respond aggressively. In the absence of such a de facto American guarantee of Iraqi state sovereignty, these trespasses could well have triggered exaggerated responses either in the form of conflict on the ground or of attempts to develop conventional military forces capable of repelling the attacks and punishing the perpetrators.

In concrete terms, without the presence of American forces, a fragile Iraqi government might well feel the need to respond forcefully to incursions. This has been the tradition in the Middle East, even though it has led to several of the region's most disastrous wars. Many Iraqi military leaders already harbor a disturbing attachment to the Iraqi military of the late 1980s—the Iraqi military that smashed Iran's ground forces and won the Iran-Iraq war. That is the same Iraqi military that threatened Syria and Israel and eventually overran Kuwait. Without an American military presence to reassure them, Iraq's political leaders might feel pressure to demonstrate to the Iraqi people that they can defend themselves. Any attempt to develop armored forces, missile forces, or attack aviation that looked like an effort to rebuild Saddam's army would set off alarm bells throughout the region, possibly stoking a regional arms race.

Conducting Counterterrorism Operations

Counterterrorism is one mission that the United States unquestionably ought to assign a lower priority going forward than it has in the past. Unfortunately, for U.S. domestic political reasons, Washington seems unlikely to do so.

Missions that support internal and regional stability and that give the United States leverage with future Iraqi governments are much more important to American security than the ability to conduct discrete counterterrorism (CT) operations within Iraq. Al-Qa'ida in Iraq (AQI) remains a threat to Iraq, but not an existential one. It also does not currently pose a significant threat to American interests outside Iraq, although it is still integrated into the regional al-Qa'ida network whose affiliates have attacked or have declared their intention to attack the United States (including al-Qa'ida in the Arabian Peninsula and in Yemen, and al-Shabaab in Somalia). AQI is severely weakened, and it is attempting to regain its footing, but whether it is able to do so will be determined as much if not more so by the course of Iraqi politics than by the successes or failures of the ISF. The ISF will undoubtedly continue to battle AQI—since 2007, Iraq has been by far the staunchest and most dedicated opponent of al-Qa'ida in the Muslim world—and will likely be able to prevent the group from reigniting sectarian civil war or toppling the government. Without American assistance, however, the Iraqi Security Forces are unlikely to be able to maintain the current pressure on AQI or finish it off (to the extent that that is even possible with a networked terrorist organization).

Numerous examples demonstrate the inability of targeted CT operations alone to degrade terrorist networks without the active and capable assistance of indigenous ground forces controlled by a competent government determined to fight the terrorists. The Yemeni government has not supported CT operations and has not worked to defeat or degrade the al-Qa'ida affiliate there. Much more limited operations in Somalia have had no discernible effect on al-Shabaab. Pakistan provides perhaps the best case in point. Islamabad has shown a real willingness and some ability to operate against al-Qa'ida itself and, supported by American clandestine operations, has done severe damage to that network. But Pakistan's leaders have been unwilling and, in some cases, unable to operate against various Taliban groups active in both Afghanistan and Pakistan, rendering American CT operations against those groups far less effective. The ability to continue to conduct targeted CT missions in Iraq is neither an effective strategy for defeating al-Qa'ida there nor a desideratum in and of itself. Sustaining the current gains against al-Qa'ida in Iraq and expanding those gains against affiliated groups there not only requires an effective military but also an Iraqi government committed to continuing the fight with its own resources as well as with outside assistance.

Even so, pure CT operations in Iraq have become secondary objectives for the United States. The principal threat to Iraq is no longer from terrorists/insurgents. The remaining terrorists remain lethal, but they no longer constitute a strategic threat to the viability of the Iraqi state. At most, they can contribute to political divisions that could constitute such a strategic threat. However, that is only a realistic possibility when Iraqis begin to blame other ethno-sectarian groups for instigating the violence, as they did in 2003–2006. Since 2008, Iraqis have tended to blame their own leaders for failing to protect them from terrorism, which demonstrates that they continue to believe that the government *can* protect them—an absolutely vital distinction, and one that the U.S. needs to continue to watch closely.

ACCEPTING RISK: FORCE PROTECTION

Force protection is not a mission, properly speaking, but a requirement of every mission. Unfortunately, it has at times become something akin to a mission—indeed, the principal mission—of U.S. forces in Iraq (and elsewhere). Whenever force protection has risen to that inappropriate level, it has been a sign that the U.S. government did not know what it was doing. *Washington cannot ignore force protection, but neither can it make it the highest priority of American forces in Iraq.*

If a military mission is truly in the vital interests of the United States, then America's military personnel will resolutely and willingly accept the risks that come with achieving that mission. If a military mission is not in the vital interests of the nation, then the government has no business asking troops to put themselves at risk, let alone accept the inevitable sacrifices it will entail. Both the Bush and Obama administrations have recognized that Iraq remains a vital interest of the United States, even if they have differed over how best to secure that vital interest. President Obama did not simply pull U.S. military forces out of Iraq, as his campaign rhetoric had seemed to suggest he would. Instead, he has repeatedly emphasized that he wants to withdraw American troops from Iraq responsibly and leave behind a stable government. As a result, far more U.S. troops will remain in Iraq for far longer than many believed when he first took office.

Nevertheless, there has already been an alarming tendency to prioritize force protection over mission fulfillment. As noted, U.S. civilian interactions with the Iraqis are dropping precipitously as a result of the shift from military-provided security to State Department-provided security, with a corresponding loss of understanding and influence, especially beyond the topmost circles of the Iraqi political elite.

The president's decision to draw down American forces in Iraq faster than the timetable required by the SA when the situation there still remains fragile and prone to a resumption of violence inherently entails a willingness to accept risk. The truly conservative (that is, risk-averse) course to take would have been to leave larger American forces in Iraq until the December 2011 deadline, push for the negotiation of a new SA, and then maintain a considerable presence for some time to ensure that when they are finally withdrawn, Iraq's political, economic, and military situations are much stronger than they are today. Thus, the administration's decision reflects a willingness to tolerate risk. This is not necessarily to find fault with that decision, it is simply to acknowledge it for what it is.

The president's decision to draw down forces from Iraq as quickly as he has chosen to do so means accepting risk in the sense that it will be impossible for the remaining U.S. forces to continue to fulfill all of the tasks they have in the past, to the same extent as in the past, and with the same safety tolerances. Something will have to give and the only question is, what? The most logical and responsible area in which to accept risk should be on matters of force protection. The remaining troops and civilians will have to complete those missions critical to U.S. vital interests and because there will be fewer of them with fewer resources at their disposal, this task will be extremely difficult. It will be impossible if force protection becomes their highest priority.

U.S. ARMS SALES TO IRAQ

Although there is some resistance, particularly in Congress, to major U.S. arms sales to Iraq, such sales could be critical to the future U.S.-Iraqi relationship. As long as Iraq desires them (which it currently does) and can afford them (which it eventually will), such arms sales, *when provided by the United States*, could be inherently stabilizing if managed effectively and in tandem with political reform in Baghdad; it could also help stabilize the region by preventing the emergence of an aggressive Iraq that would pose a threat to its neighbors. In addition, arms sales represent yet another source of influence with the Iraqi leadership since American arms are items Baghdad greatly desires. Consequently, these sales should be considered from a strategic perspective, not a commercial one.

As with all American interactions toward Iraq in future, however, Washington's critical consideration when weighing arms sales to Iraq must be their impact on Iraq's domestic politics. Again, such sales can be extremely helpful in this area, as we discuss below. However, they can also be destabilizing if mishandled. Moreover, they too represent a critical element of American leverage with Iraq. In particular, American arms sales to Iraq should be conditioned on continuing improvement (or at least no significant deterioration) in Iraq's civil-military relations. The Iraqi military should understand that Washington's willingness to provide the arms they so desperately want will be possible only to the extent that the ISF stays in its lane and stays out of politics. So too should the government understand that American arms sales—among other things—will be jeopardized by efforts to politicize the ISF. Finally, because the KRG is terrified that the central government will imagine it has a military "solution" to their dispute once the ISF is armed with American tanks and fighter-bombers, Washington must lay down clear red lines to both sides regarding what is permissible. Furthermore, the United States should extract guarantees from the government that it will not invade the Kurdistan region, except perhaps in the highly unlikely event that the Kurds unilaterally declare independence from Iraq or use their own forces to attack other parts of Iraq.

The Utility of American Arms Sales to Iraq

The more that the United States remains Iraq's paramount military partner, the less likely (or even able) the Iraqi armed forces will be to threaten neighboring states. The modern military history of the Arab world makes clear that Arab allies of the United States become completely dependent on the United States and lose the capacity to project power without American support (and therefore approval).[4] Today, Jordan, Egypt, and all of the GCC states coordinate all of their major, external military activities with the United States. They rarely try to project power beyond their borders because they are effectively unable to do so without American support; a situation deepened by their tendency to buy weapons platforms at the expense of logistics and other support functions. Moreover, on a number of occasions, Washington has been able to prevent its Middle Eastern allies from launching military operations because of these countries' dependence on the United States. Such was not the experience of Arab states that relied on the Soviet Union, China, or other countries for their military support, and today there is little to suggest that Russia, China, or any other country would even try to use their arms sales to head off a war.

For this reason, Washington should welcome Iraq's desire to develop a long-term military-to-military relationship and buy American weaponry. Iraq's generals would like to return to the glory days of 1988-1990, but one thing that they do not want to recreate, if they can avoid it, is their reliance on Soviet military hardware. Iraqis have long recognized that Western (particularly American) weaponry is superior, and as such, they have coveted it. Since the fall of Saddam and the Iraqi military's subsequent exposure to the U.S. military, that desire has only grown. It should also be noted that there is not any perception on the part of Iraqi generals and their political counterparts that the United States is forcing them to buy American materiel as payback for America's efforts in rebuilding the country. Rather, the Iraqis *want* American equipment. By the same token, they are quick to point out that if the United States won't sell them what they want, they will go elsewhere and with their oil money, they will find Russian, Chinese, European, or other sellers.

For their part, GCC rulers also want to see a close military-to-military relationship continue between the United States and Iraq, coupled with large-scale arms sales. More than anyone else, the GCC states recognize that reliance on American arms and American training and assistance makes their militaries *dependent* on the United States for logistical support, intelligence, command and control, and a variety of other requirements. GCC officials say quite openly, albeit only in private, that an extensive Iraqi-American arms and security relationship is the best insurance they can get that Iraq will never threaten their countries with its conventional might again.

Moreover, refusing Iraq one of the most important benefits that many other American partners and allies receive will seriously undermine America's ability to influence Iraq in the future. Excluding Iraq from a key security benefit that so many other U.S. allies receive is as clear a statement as America could possibly make that it does not regard Iraq as a partner, let alone an ally, and that Iraq is outside America's sphere of interest. If the Obama administration carries through on its discussions about establishing a long-term security relationship with Afghanistan, the point will be made even more sharply. The White House will have no basis to complain when Iraq's leaders make strategic calculations to America's disadvantage if the U.S. has thus explicitly communicated its lack of interest in Iraq's security and, in fact, its belief in Iraq's fundamental unimportance to American security interests.

The one important caveat to this overarching point is cost. Iraq may someday be a very rich country thanks to its oil reserves, which only seem to grow by the day. Today, however, Iraq is a very poor country, with a GDP per capita of only $3,800 (ranking it 160th in the world) and massive budgetary needs compared to the revenues available. From a financial perspective, multi-million dollar fighter aircraft are a luxury that Iraq cannot currently afford. Even politically, Iraq's people seem far more interested in investing in their economy than in fancy new weapons. Consequently, the U.S. interest in preventing domestic political problems means keeping Iraqi military spending circumscribed so that it does not bankrupt the country and preclude critical expenditures on basic needs and economic development.

It is worth pointing out that this is yet another reason for the United States to aggressively seek to be Iraq's primary arms supplier. Simply put, no other country is likely to care about Iraq's finances the way that the United States does. Iraq's leadership is determined to buy these big-ticket weapons systems, and they have repeatedly stated that they would buy them from Europe, Russia, or China if they cannot get them from the United States. Certainly Russia and China would not care whether Iraq is spending too much on their arms, and European nations may only to the extent that the United States pressures them. Only Washington will urge Iraq to spend less, work with Iraq to spread out its arms purchases over longer stretches of time, and otherwise ensure that defense spending does not come at the cost of financial stability.

THE IMPORTANCE OF A NEW SECURITY AGREEMENT

The withdrawal of American military forces from Iraq has been the central feature of President Obama's Iraq policy. This complicates American policy toward Iraq moving forward, but it does not end it. America's vital interests will endure, and the president has also demonstrated a strong desire to secure those interests even as he draws down U.S. force levels. Indeed, President Obama has repeatedly signaled a willingness to go slower than theoretically possible to preserve forces on hand to prevent Iraq's collapse, to give the Iraqis a reasonable chance to build on their progress so far, and to allow the United States to continue to play an active role in Iraq to help the Iraqis reach the stability that both Americans and they seek.

The foregoing discussion should make clear that American troops continue to play important roles in Iraq which are critical not only to Iraqi interests, but to U.S. interests as well. Virtually every mission described above could still be performed at even lower troop levels, albeit inevitably with correspondingly more modest impact and greater risks. As long as Iraq continues to make progress, such shifts should be acceptable in time. Nevertheless, it is hard to imagine that Iraq will progress so rapidly that American troops will not be needed at all to perform any of these missions in the next several years. It seems far more likely that several thousands—perhaps even tens of thousands—will still be needed until at least the middle of the decade.

That means that the United States and Iraq will need to come to an agreement on a new status of forces agreement (SOFA) to follow the expiration of the current SA at the end of 2011. That may not be easy. First, there are many Iraqi politicians who understand the importance of the American military presence, but have proven unwilling to publicly advocate for it. Many Iraqi politicians fear being painted as American puppets and betrayers of Iraqi sovereignty if they openly support a continued American military presence. Some Iraqis maintain that the absence of a validating referendum makes the current agreement illegal.

Perhaps of much greater danger in the future, some Iraqi politicians—particularly those in power—may see the American presence as doing more harm than good to their own personal interests. Some groups may see the United States as a hindrance to their acting or exercising power as they see fit. That is, they may not want to be forced to respect the rule of law and other constitutional niceties, and they may therefore want to end the American military presence in Iraq to remove a principal bar to such actions.

It is in part for this reason that the United States cannot want a new status of forces agreement more than the Iraqis themselves. It is certainly true that, as we have argued repeatedly, the United States has vital interests in Iraq independent of those of the Iraqis or their leadership. But in an era in which the United States has already relinquished its role as occupier, restored sovereignty and other prerogatives to the Iraqis, and announced that its primary goal is to leave, there is a limit to what the United States can do. As we also noted above, the United States still has a great deal of influence with Iraq, but it is influence, not control. The United States cannot force the Iraqis to agree to a new SOFA, let alone one entirely based on American terms.

There are three crucial, interrelated rules the United States should observe when negotiating a new SOFA with Iraq:

1. The United States must have a new SOFA with Iraq that preserves the ability of American forces to serve as peacekeepers and as the ultimate guardian of Iraqi rule of law. The United States must be able to maintain stability in Iraq, and deter or prevent the worst government abuses, if necessary. An American presence cannot become a fiction, or a façade to cover up an increasingly violent and abusive political system.

2. The Iraqis must understand that the entire Strategic Framework Agreement—which covers all U.S. military, political, economic, and diplomatic aid to Iraq—is tied to the signing of a new SOFA, and a new SOFA that meets American needs. This is the greatest source of leverage the United States has, and it must be employed to secure what is of greatest importance to American interests in Iraq.

3. The United States must be ready to walk away from Iraq altogether if the government of Iraq is unwilling to agree to such a SOFA.

It is unlikely that the Obama administration will be able to walk back the terms that the Bush team agreed to in late 2008 for the current Security Agreement, but they should not accept any less and should be willing to wash their hands of Iraq altogether if the Iraqis refuse. The rationale is brutal, but compelling: *Any Iraqi government that is not interested in some kind of adequate American military presence after 2011—or a U.S. military presence that can continue to act as the guarantor of Iraqi stability and its continued development as a democracy—is not a government that the United States should want to support.* Such an Iraqi government is bound to act in ways that will jeopardize, if not deliberately subvert, Iraq's democracy and ultimately its stability. It may do so out of political weakness, or misperceived strength, but the result will be the same.

THE DURATION OF AN AMERICAN MILITARY PRESENCE IN IRAQ

Even if the Iraqi government does request that the United States retain troops in Iraq beyond the expiration of the current Security Agreement in December 2011, it may ask Washington for its assessment of how many and for how long those troops should remain. Any status of forces agreement that succeeded the current Security Agreement, would likely have to include some provisions related to these questions. However, the United States ought to stress the desirability of leaving any restrictions as ambiguous as possible.

As we have noted several times, as long as Iraq continues to make progress—slow and stumbling though it may be—the United States should be able to further draw down its forces from the current 50,000-man level. Indeed, some considerable reductions should be possible if all that happens in Iraq is that there is no marked *increase* in violence. Some of the troops employed in counterterrorism missions could be redeployed elsewhere, and even some peacekeeping missions might be thinned out (although Washington must always remember that peacekeeping is now the highest priority of U.S. forces in Iraq). Beyond that, it is much harder to speculate because the number of American troops that would be preferable to maintain in Iraq can only be measured by the state of Iraq's security, as well as by the economic and (of greatest importance) political situation. These are impossible to predict at this point because of the enormous uncertainties involved. In other words, a U.S. troop withdrawal would need to be conditions-based rather than tied to a specific timetable.

CHAPTER FOUR

Governance and Economics

Perhaps nowhere else have U.S. goals and interests in Iraq changed more over the last several years than in the economics and governance sphere. The Bush administration's need to justify the invasion of Iraq gave it a compelling interest in turning Iraq into a functional, thriving democracy. This then required that Iraq progress in virtually every sector. Even later, during the period of the surge, when Washington's goal was first and foremost to prevent Iraq's descent into an all-consuming civil war, the United States still needed the Iraqi governmental and economic structures to function properly to undermine support for the insurgents and militia and secure popular support for the revived and revised American effort. For six years, the United States desperately needed Iraq to improve virtually every aspect of its governmental and economic performance to meet American needs.

This changed fundamentally with the signing of the 2009 Security Agreement, which both formally and psychologically transferred primary responsibility for Iraq's fate from Washington to Baghdad. At the same time, the new Obama administration's desire to eliminate the U.S. military presence from Iraq—and to otherwise diminish American involvement there—fundamentally altered the landscape.

Moreover, the outbreak of democratic ideas across Iraq has meant that average Iraqis now blame their own government for failures in governance and the economy (and security as well). Consequently, better governmental and economic performance is now something that the Iraqi government desperately needs for its own interests—to maintain its legitimacy in the broadest sense, and for individual politicians to win and hold power in the narrowest. Progress on governance and economics has largely switched from being something that the U.S. needs the Iraqis to do for American interests, to being something that the Iraqis need help doing for their own interests.

To a great extent, then, assistance to the Iraqi government (both central and local) and economy is no longer a vital American need in Iraq. However, that blanket statement requires two immediate, crucial caveats. First, there are certain aspects of governance and the economy that are directly relevant to vital American interests, particularly any aspect of either that could lead to the kind of collapse that would trigger a civil war. Iraq's oil and water sectors stand out in this area, but it is also the case that overall the United States cannot allow the Iraqi economy to fall so far that unemployment prompts massive internal unrest, as happened to a certain extent in 2005–2006. Second, the United States must always keep in mind that even those aspects of governance and the economy that are not of direct importance to American interests can still have an important indirect role if they are areas of importance to Iraq's political leadership. Like the provision of combat enablers to the ISF, anything that the Iraqis want and that the United States can provide has the potential to increase American leverage over Iraq's domestic politics—the center of gravity for American interests in Iraq, where the fate of Iraq will ultimately be determined, and where the United States needs as much leverage as possible to help Iraq's fractious leadership steer the country on a course toward long-term stability and democracy.

The consolidation of a stable, democratic Iraq depends in particular upon the evolution of a government that is seen as legitimate and effective and the development of an economy that provides opportunities and livelihoods to Iraq's young and fast-growing population. After the provision of basic security, the two most critical standards by which the political system will be judged are the delivery of essential services, especially electricity, and increased employment. The provision of basic services and jobs has been a consistent demand of the Iraqi population since the fall of Saddam Husayn's regime, and a source of constant criticism of the government. Baghdad's failure to deliver these basic goods could cause increasing social and political unrest, as seen in protests over electricity shortages in July and August of 2010. At the same time, the Iraqi economy is simply not generating enough jobs to accommodate the approximately 450,000 Iraqis who enter the labor force each year,[1] a critical trend that could be exacerbated by the effects of growing water scarcity on the agriculture sector (traditionally Iraq's main private sector employer). Taken together, a governance failure in these two areas—services and the economy—could discredit Iraq's democracy and raise the risk that non-democratic alternatives may emerge.

Although is it unquestionably of vital importance to Iraq's economy, it is therefore possible that too much U.S. attention has been directed toward oil production levels. Iraqi authorities have clear incentives to increase oil production and, as demonstrated by the two licensing rounds held in 2009, are taking concrete steps to do so.

Instead, the fundamental governance and economic challenge in Iraq is to improve the efficiency and transparency of the processes that transform a barrel of oil sold into the goods and services that the Iraqi public desires—like increased electricity output, water and sewage networks, roads, schools, health clinics, and job opportunities.[2] Here, Iraq already suffers from the oil curse, with development of the hydrocarbons sector far outpacing other important areas of the economy, and providing a large source of rent. Iraq's oil wealth has been a source of endemic corruption which most Iraqis see as the principal cause of poor service delivery[3] and a political economy heavily tilted toward the public sector. This has resulted in the lowest employment-to-population ratio in the region.[4] The foremost goal of

U.S. economic and governance assistance to Iraq should therefore be to ameliorate the most pernicious effects of the oil curse by conditioning economic assistance on the willingness of the Iraqi government to improve its transparency, oversight, and accountability mechanisms.

THE STRATEGIC FRAMEWORK AGREEMENT AND U.S. PRIORITIES

In the Strategic Framework Agreement (SFA), the United States and Iraq have a basic scaffolding for a long-term partnership for building "a diversified and advanced economy" and "strengthening and developing democracy in Iraq." The SFA, which was an Iraqi idea and something that the Iraqis requested of the United States as a companion to the Security Agreement, was intended to make the continued U.S. presence more politically palatable by promoting U.S. investment in Iraq and demonstrating that the U.S.-Iraqi partnership was not limited to the security realm. Given the force of Iraqi nationalism, it is vital to the future of the U.S.-Iraqi partnership, including in the security realm, that the Iraqis perceive value from the implementation of the SFA. It is also the case that if the United States wants to maintain leverage in the Iraqi domestic political arena, the SFA must deliver outcomes that Iraqis want.

The central challenge will be reconciling U.S. and Iraqi expectations for the SFA and finding creative ways to use it to pursue these critical aims in an era of sharply declining resources. *The United States will need to be upfront with the Iraqi government that the SFA does not represent a new Marshall Plan for Iraq and that it will only be making relatively limited additional financial contributions to Iraq's reconstruction.*[5] This will doubtless be a major disappointment for many Iraqis who imagine still more largesse flowing their way from the U.S. Treasury. To mitigate this disappointment and to make the American contribution to the SFA desirable to Iraqis, the United States will have to think creatively about how to provide valuable assistance without the need for large-scale American financing.

Moreover, as Iraq's oil revenues increase over time, Iraq should be able to pay for more of its reconstruction needs. Therefore, the real value added from the American side will be insight and advice on how best to employ those resources rather than adding in more resources—something that neither the administration nor Congress has any interest in providing.

Consequently, the United States should focus the assistance it provides to Iraq under the rubric of the SFA primarily on capacity building by providing technical advice, consulting services, and technology and knowledge transfers to key areas of the Iraqi economy. The United States must now consider both how it can be most effective in this role and how it can maintain the leverage to encourage Iraqis to build a transparent and accountable government when America is no longer putting up large amounts of its own money for projects.

There are, fortunately, a number of areas of the Iraqi economy both inside and outside the SFA where the United States can deliver tangible added value at a relatively low financial cost. These include:

—International engagement and mediation on issues such as Iraq's Chapter VII UN obligations, including annual reparations to Kuwait and disputes over the Iraq-Kuwait maritime boundary (which have the potential to hamper Iraq's primary oil export route through the Persian Gulf),[6] dialogue with Iraq's northern neighbors, especially Turkey, on regional water-sharing agreements, and the protection of Iraq's oil revenues from legal claims relating to actions of the former regime, something that if left unaddressed could hamper long-term investment in the oil and gas sector;

—Formation of a joint economic commission under the SFA, which, when requested by Iraqis, could serve as a central oversight body to coordinate, monitor, and provide technical expertise for reconstruction and capital investment projects initiated with Iraqi funds;

—Technical advice, knowledge sharing, and technology transfer to vital areas of the Iraqi economy and society such as improved domestic water efficiency and management and agricultural development and productivity;

—Finding ways to continue to assist Iraq's provincial governments, even after the shutting down of U.S.-led Provincial Reconstruction Teams (PRTs), in obtaining the release of their annual investment budget allocations from national authorities; and

—Legislative actions to create a business environment that encourages Western business investments.

The United States should make it clear that assistance of this type is contingent upon Iraqi authorities at both the national and provincial level taking specific steps to put in place transparency, oversight, and accountability mechanisms aimed at mitigating the corrupting and insulating effects of Iraq's oil economy. Fortunately, and not by coincidence, these actions are all fully consistent with the goals of the new Iraqi National Development Plan to halve unemployment, promote rural development, increase environmental protection, reform administrative systems, and support decentralization. They would also be of substantial financial and even political benefit to Iraq's new government and generally should not be provided until it demonstrates the willingness to take the hard steps to enable a greater portion of Iraq's oil wealth to be turned into investments that fuel service delivery, economic growth, and broader political legitimacy. This must ultimately be the overriding objective of all U.S. economic and governance assistance to Iraq.

OIL: COMBATING THE CURSE

Development of the oil and gas sector is critical to the Iraqi economy and its finances. The hydrocarbon sector accounts for approximately two-thirds of GDP and 90 percent of government revenues, and it will be the main source of government funds and of economic growth for years to come. While Iraq has aspirations to diversify its economy and progress with a massive reconstruction plan, all of these ambitions are premised on expanding oil and gas output and exports. The model in Iraqi eyes is the producing states of the Persian Gulf, with

Iraq's political leaders looking to Abu Dhabi in particular as a source of reference.

Over the past seven years, U.S. policy has focused on developing the oil and gas sector, and filling Iraqi coffers. Iraq sits on a massive base of proven oil resources, now estimated officially at 143 billion barrels. Its undiscovered volumes may match that figure, potentially putting Iraq on par with Saudi Arabia in terms of crude oil reserves. Iraq's production potential is far higher than anything the country has experienced in the past. Just the fields awarded in the two licensing rounds held in 2009 have the potential to add 9.5 million barrels per day of output to the 2.3 million barrels per day currently being produced (although it is clear that the oil markets cannot absorb these volumes quickly without experiencing a price crash, something Iraq wants to avoid). Add other fields that Iraq is looking to develop itself, unexplored acreage (including reservoirs under presently producing fields), and production from the Kurdistan region, and that output figure climbs even higher. Iraq's potential is not limited by its resource base, but by its capacity to manage the development of this base effectively.

The number of licenses—and scale of the fields involved—awarded last year illustrates Iraq's ambitions. Political leaders are clearly eying the massive revenue windfall that these developments will eventually bring (although the scale of Iraq's existing structural budget deficit, and the likely costs of additional infrastructure—export pipelines, power generation, water provision—needed to make these oil projects fully viable will keep Iraqi finances tight for the first few years). Moreover, leaders in Baghdad are keenly aware of the shift in the regional balance of power that a large increase in Iraqi output would lead to. If the country can develop large volumes of spare capacity (akin to Saudi Arabia's), it will position itself as a global player able to be a potential price maker in oil markets.

But it is not just a matter of developing these oil resources that will be important. In domestic political terms, it is the capacity to use the revenue generated by rising exports effectively to meet services, employment, infrastructure, and economic diversification needs that will be important. The anticipated windfall, which the local economy will struggle to absorb, combined with weak institutions and often ineffective government, could easily distort the Iraqi economy, hamper diversification efforts, and provide the basis for a return to greater authoritarianism in the future. Even at present production levels, the state is struggling to spend its budget, corruption is ever-more rife, and representative politics is being undermined (the drawn-out crisis over government formation was arguably facilitated in part because the political elite had access to a ready source of revenues that allowed them to at least maintain important patronage networks, even if overall management of the country suffered).

Iraq's challenge moving forward is therefore not revenue generation, but developing effective and transparent institutions and frameworks for spending that revenue. And in many ways, the U.S. faces a race against time to be able to influence Iraqi decisionmakers toward this end. Given nationalist sensitivities, the options open to Washington are relatively limited; in fact, they always were. Proposals to privatize the sector, or schemes to distribute payments directly to the population as a means of promoting private consumption and investment were pipedreams. Iraq not only has a tradition of state management of the sector, but political leaders recognize the power that this authority bestows and have always been reluctant to give it up. As the coffers grow, this determination to remain in control will only increase.

But that is not to say that U.S. policymakers do not have options to influence Iraqi behavior and encourage high levels of transparency. Two areas of potential leverage are Iraq's continued Chapter VII UN obligations and reparations commitments, and outstanding claims against the government dating back to Saddam Husayn's regime. In the case of the former, the Iraqi government is clearly keen to lessen the reparations burden, even as it anticipates higher overall revenues. However, efforts so far to reach a deal with Kuwait have foundered, in part over continued disputes over border demarcation. One option for Washington would be to engage more actively in mediation of this issue, but make its efforts contingent on an Iraqi commitment to maintain a successor to the current Development Fund for Iraq (something that Baghdad is already establishing) and ensure that revenue flows are transparent and subject to regular auditing by an independent body, akin to the current International Advisory and Monetary Board, which presently plays that role.

The area of claims offers U.S. policymakers an opportunity for exerting leverage over Baghdad. Until now, Iraqi oil exports have been protected against attachment claims (claims to Iraqi oil exports from parties that have claims against the Iraqi government stemming from the Saddam era) by UN Security Council resolutions and U.S. executive orders. However, the former could lapse by June 30, 2011, when the mandate for the Development Fund for Iraq is scheduled to end, and it would take a new Security Council resolution to replace it. Meanwhile, Washington's jurisdiction ended with the Security Agreement in 2008.

Yet, Article 26 of the SA provides a potential avenue for greater U.S. involvement in assisting Iraq in protecting itself against such claims (and indeed in resolving the reparations issue). The article pledges U.S. support for Iraqi efforts to mitigate attachment risks: "The United States shall remain fully and actively engaged with the Government of Iraq with respect to continuation of such protections [of oil export revenue] and with respect to such claims." This language provides a foundation for more active initiatives by the U.S. executive branch. Washington could promise more robust diplomatic and mediation efforts to convince allied governments to take measures to protect Iraqi assets against attachment, possibly through the UN Security Council.

Either of these avenues could provide a card to play in encouraging Iraq to be more transparent in its collection of oil revenue and in its spending. But ultimately the limits on U.S. influence must be recognized; Washington is in no position to demand, merely to negotiate.

Still, if Washington wants to play this card, it should do so sooner rather than later because there are a number of factors that make this issue time-sensitive, not least the concerns of international oil and gas companies about attachment risks, given their preference for payment in oil as proposed by the Ministry of Oil rather than in cash. As time goes by, Iraq—by dint of its increased revenues and precedent—is likely to be in a stronger position to brush off U.S. pressure for transparency. Thus, early moves by Washington are likely to be the most fruitful.

WATER: THE BATTLE AHEAD

Iraq's extreme dependence on its oil sector is frequently remarked upon, but the country's development and stability is no less dependent upon another critical natural resource: water. This has been true for thousands of years. Modern-day Iraq roughly corresponds to historical Mesopotamia, literally "the land between the two rivers"—the eastern half of the Fertile Crescent between the Tigris and the Euphrates. While the Middle East is one of the most water-scarce regions in the world, Iraq has historically been blessed with an abundance of water flowing through these two great river systems. As a result, it is one of the few countries in the region where large-scale irrigation and agri-business is possible. Iraq's once-legendary agricultural sector has traditionally been a source of stability, serving as a major source of employment and food for the Middle East. The importance of water to Iraq's society and economy extends well beyond agriculture however. Hydroelectric power has contributed as much as 20 percent of Iraq's energy requirements in some years, and water also plays an important role in industry, including the oil sector, which requires large volumes of water injections to maintain the pressure necessary to extract oil from producing wells.[7] Finally, water is of course essential for drinking and sanitation purposes.

It should therefore be a matter of real concern both to Iraq and the United States that over the last decade Iraq has faced water shortages unparalleled in its long history. These are a result of several inter-related factors that include: lower than average rainfall over the last ten years (including a severe multi-year drought that has been going on since 2007); a sharp reduction in water flows in the Tigris and Euphrates due to upstream dam construction in Turkey, Syria, and Iran; and major inefficiencies in domestic water usage that have origins in both hardware (war-damaged infrastructure and poor maintenance) and software problems (general governance disruption and declining water management technocratic capacity). Compounding these negative trends is the country's young and rapidly growing population, which is expected to contribute to rising water demand in the future. The net result of lowering supply and rising demand may be a severe water crisis that has the potential to cause population displacement, internal instability, and a level of discontent with government that could have profound consequences for Iraq's future. Water disputes have also become a serious source of political tension with Iraq's upstream neighbors, principally Turkey.

According to data from the Iraqi Ministry of Water Resources, from 1990 to 2007 Iraq received only 80 percent of the average annual flow of 77 billion cubic meters (BCM) that the Tigris and Euphrates supplied between 1930 and 1990 (and these figures do not reflect the severe drought that began in 2007). The Iraqi Minister of Water Resources has described the problem with the Euphrates as particularly acute, stating that as a result of almost thirty dams built upstream (mostly in Turkey), Iraq now receives ten to fifteen BCM per year from the Euphrates as compared to thirty BCM during the 1980s.[8] Similar problems could occur with the Tigris if Turkey's Ilisu Dam project goes ahead, which some Iraqi water officials estimate would result in the flow of the Tigris into Iraq being halved.[9] Already, low water volumes have contributed to increased water and soil salinity, expanded desertification in a country where only 10 percent to 15 percent of the land is classified as arable, record low agricultural outputs, serious water quality issues in several Iraqi cities such as Basra, and reduced hydropower generation at a time of a national electricity crisis. At the same time, limited progress has been made in addressing regional water issues, with a meeting of Iraqi, Turkish, and Syrian water ministers in September 2009 proving inconclusive. Turkey's upstream geographical position and political standing in the region makes it unlikely that its current policy stance of ruling out an increase in water delivery to its downstream neighbors will change absent greater geopolitical leverage or wider international pressure.[10]

Some fear that Iraq's next series of conflict could be fought over water. As Iraq's already poverty stricken rural areas struggle with water shortages, substantial additional displacement to its cities could create an unstable situation of rural migrants increasingly competing with urban dwellers for already scarce employment opportunities. A 2009 UNESCO study found that over 100,000 people in northern Iraq have been forced to evacuate their homes since water supplies began to dwindle in 2005,[11] while Iraqi government estimates indicate that up to 30,000 more may have left the Shatt al-Arab marshes in southern Iraq due to increasing water and soil salinity. It is worth recognizing that sudden, rapid urbanization of this sort has frequently produced internal unrest and even revolution or civil war in many countries—including Iraq itself in the 1950s. In the rural areas of central and southern Iraq, tense negotiations and conflicts between upstream and downstream tribes over scarce water resources have been reported. Similarly, the assassinations of local irrigation officials have been attributed to the government's inability to effectively manage the acute nationwide water shortage.[12]

The water crisis falls into the category of issues that the next Iraqi government will be forced to confront at an early stage as opposed to at a time of its choosing. The caretaker Ministries of Water Resources, Foreign Affairs, Planning, and Agriculture established a Water Committee in August 2010, but will be unable to take long-term steps in the absence of a government. It is likely that the way in which the new government handles this crisis will have a major impact on how the Iraqi public perceives its competence, and a failure to adequately come to grips with water problems over the next three to four years could unacceptably raise the risk of a serious long-term economic downturn and rapid displacement from rural areas. Some of the greatest potential for instability in this respect is in what is likely to be a Shi'i-led government's primary base of support—the mainly Shi'i southern Iraq, which is the area furthest downstream and consequently suffering some of the greatest problems with water pollution and salinity levels. *It is in the clear interest of the United States to provide support to the government of Iraq regarding water management because it will be of substantial value to Iraqi leaders and because it is an issue that has the potential to cause instability that could result in a civil war.*

United States support to Iraq in confronting its water crisis should proceed along three lines:

—While its potential leverage in this area is limited, the United States or United Nations could help Iraq, Turkey, and Syria create regional forums and technical dialogues aimed at promoting more stable and predictable regional trans-boundary water management.[13] In particular, Turkey has strong trade and energy interests in Iraq that water disputes could jeopardize[14] and the United States could help its two allies talk to each other on these issues.

—Drought and regional factors are major drivers of water scarcity in Iraq, but domestic factors play a role as well. Iraq urgently needs to increase its water efficiency across irrigation, agricultural, industrial, and household uses. As such, technical assistance and knowledge transfers to Iraqi authorities in integrated water sector planning, water allocation and distribution, designing incentives for water conservation, desalinization projects, and developing effective infrastructure operations and maintenance programs should be a major focus on U.S. economic cooperation with Iraq.

—Agriculture accounts for about 75 percent of Iraq's water use, is the country's number-one private-sector employer, and the second largest contributor to GDP after oil.[15] However, there has been limited investment in the sector's technology, infrastructure, and knowledge transfer over the last several decades, which has led to reduced production and productivity. This has been a factor in bringing about increasing food insecurity in rural areas, urban migration, greater unemployment, and even social unrest in Iraqi cities during the 1990s. In particular, Iraqi farmers overwhelmingly rely on inundation agricultural techniques that consume huge amounts of freshwater. If Iraqi farmers could be convinced and assisted to abandon this ancient method, Iraq's water needs could be greatly reduced and its water problems might even be eliminated altogether. Unfortunately, for several years, American officials have been trying to convince the Iraqi government to adopt a program that would help Iraqi farmers to shift away from inundation agriculture without luck. *The United States, particularly the U.S. Department of Agriculture, should press Baghdad to institute a nationwide program to transition away from inundation agriculture.* Washington should further assist Iraq's Ministry of Agriculture to revitalize or develop various capabilities, including effective planning, equitable distribution of resources, modernization of infrastructure, improvement of the quality of agricultural products, and fostering of technology transfers to increase productivity and yields.

Agriculture and water are key areas where the governments of Iraq and the United States can produce tangible results, demonstrate to the Iraqi people that Iraqi and American officials care about their prosperity, and underscore the value of the Strategic Framework partnership. Indeed, PRT officials have indicated that U.S. Department of Agriculture technical experts have been the most widely and enthusiastically accepted members of PRT teams by their Iraqi counterparts. From a U.S. interest standpoint, this assistance can also be a source of leverage. Iraq likely needs more help from the United States with developing its water infrastructure and agricultural sector than it does with improving the country's oil sector, and this assistance should be once again conditioned on progress in Iraqi domestic politics and the implementation of broader accountability and oversight mechanisms aimed at combating corruption within the Iraqi government.

THE PROVINCES: MAKING DECENTRALIZATION WORK

Outside of the Kurdistan region, Iraq had extremely limited experience with genuine local autonomy prior to 2003. Local government, including the current provincial council and governor structures, remains a new concept. In fact, local capacity had to be created in some places where none had existed before. The consolidation of the provincial government experiment is strategically significant to Iraq's stability because it offers a practical alternative to the politically controversial extremes of the excessive concentration of power in Baghdad and the formation of a host of new fully autonomous regions in central and southern Iraq. More generally, as is the case at the national level, improving the quality of provincial governance is important in countering potential feelings of disillusionment and disenfranchisement with government among the Iraqi public. This may be particularly the case in scenarios where the national government is not perceived as representative or being accommodating of minority groups such as Sunni Arabs.

The 2008 Provincial Powers Law, which took effect everywhere except in Kirkuk and the Kurdistan region's three governorates after the January 2009 provincial elections, provided Iraq's provincial governments with relatively limited authorities, such as issuing local laws and regulations, approving the security plans in the province, preparing and executing the province's general budget, and coordinating policies with the provincial directorates (offices) of national ministries. The provinces' general budgets are currently limited to funds provided in the federal budget, and are meant for implementing one-year capital investment projects (about $2 billion per year is split among the fifteen non-KRG governorates based on population ratios).[16] The Provincial Powers Law did *not* alter existing practices of the local justice, education, health, municipalities and public works, and transport directorates being administered, funded, and controlled by their respective federal line ministries. When combined with the reality that the federal Iraqi Army and federal police continue to be extensively deployed nationwide as a domestic counterinsurgency force, provincial governments in fact have relatively circumscribed formal roles outside of planning and executing their annual investment budget (anecdotally some governors are able to exert greater authority depending on the strength of their personal networks in the governorate). Given that the United States has an interest in Iraqi government being seen as legitimate and effective regardless of the level, it is important that provincial governments deliver on this one area where they have direct responsibility: executing provincial budgets to deliver road, sanitation, electricity, and school projects that match local needs.

Since November 2005, U.S. Provincial Reconstruction Teams (PRTs) have been deployed in Iraq's fifteen governorates and the Kurdistan region. While criticized early on for lacking clearly integrated strategies and goals, the PRTs have grown into an interagency platform for U.S. government operations in the provinces. They have generally focused on promoting provincial budget execution, increasing local government capacity to deliver basic services, and playing a valuable political reporting and diplomatic outreach role. The PRTs have for some time concentrated upon capacity building and technical advice to provincial councils rather than providing funding or implementing "bricks and mortar" reconstruction projects. Their signature focus has appropriately been directed to the one tangible authority possessed by the provincial councils—budget execution—and the PRTs have contributed to the substantial increase in provincial budget execution rates since provincial investment funds were first allocated beginning with Iraq's 2006 federal budget.[17] The PRTs accomplished this by working with provincial leaders to create detailed budgets that are itemized by sector and district while providing basic design tools for project and implementation, stressing detailed planning, promoting a transparent bidding process, working with provincial governments to publish ledgers of implemented projects, and pushing for provincial council oversight of the process (rather than it just being left to governors). This type of budget planning capacity could become even more relevant if provisions in Iraq's 2010 budget are implemented to pay oil-producing provinces a royalty per barrel of crude oil produced, per barrel of oil refined, or per 150 cubic meters of natural gas produced and to also pay provinces with holy sites a fee (currently, twenty dollars) per religious pilgrim who visits.

Looking forward, the challenge is to identify key PRT functions that can continue as overall U.S. assistance is steadily reduced and the teams themselves are shuttered. The PRTs are currently scheduled to operate until mid-2011, although this will depend upon the pace of the U.S. drawdown, as most PRTs rely heavily on the military for security and life support. The PRTs will be replaced by two consulates in al-Basrah and Irbil, as well as regional embassy offices in Kirkuk and Mosul. The PRTs' work on governance and rule of law, economic development, education and culture, and public health will be transitioned to national USAID and U.S. Department of Agriculture (USDA) programs. The PRTs' current priority is aimed at ensuring that core concepts of governance and rule of law are grasped by their provincial counterparts before the handover occurs. This transition will inevitably result in reduced U.S. visibility into political developments in the provinces, while the USAID implementing partner model will not (and it is not intended to) deliver the same American diplomatic outreach that State Department–led PRTs provide. In particular, the United States will have no permanent civilian presence between Basra and Baghdad—the Shi'i heartland of Iraq, despite a determined campaign by the leadership of the city of Najaf to have a consulate established there as well. (As an aside, because of the importance of the city of Najaf as the spiritual capital of the Shi'i world, the Obama administration would do well to reexamine its current plans and make provisions for a consulate in Najaf as well.)

While the political and diplomatic function of the PRTs appears to be an unavoidable casualty of the drawdown, the United States must now understand what PRT functions are most valued by Iraqis and how such programs can be utilized to create incentives for properly planned and transparent provincial budgeting. In doing so, the United States needs to recall that budget execution remains the one concrete litmus test of the long-term provincial government capacity and performance. The PRTs' counterparts on the Iraqi side are reported to have seen the teams primarily as a source of money and projects, or as a means of squeezing funds out of Baghdad.[18] However, USAID and other government departments, such as the USDA, are likely to be better equipped to take over economic development and agricultural, health, and economic technical assistance functions than it is to fill the "connective tissue" role that the PRTs played to help provincial councils overcome roadblocks in getting provincial funds released from national actors.

USAID and the broader U.S. government should therefore prioritize focused capacity-building and technical assistance efforts aimed at promoting provincial budget execution, and in particular the release of investments funds to the provinces by the federal Ministries of Planning and Finance. This is something that is in the U.S. interest (because it is necessary for provincial governments to be successful) and something that provincial councils value (help in getting access to their funds). The regrettably discontinued Department of Defense's Provincial Procurement Assistance Teams (PPAT) are an example of implementing partner models with largely Iraqi teams that could function in a post-PRT environment and contribute to this goal.[19] Such programs should be maintained in the face of declining resources, but also be conditioned upon provincial councils continuing the planning, reporting, oversight, and transparency systems that the PRTs and USAID have already worked to establish for the provincial budget execution process. Similarly, the United States should view the limited provincial reconstruction projects it continues to fund as means to buy accountability and oversight mechanisms at the local levels.

CHAPTER FIVE

REGIONAL ISSUES

For many years, the United States strove mightily to enlist the efforts of Iraq's neighbors to help stabilize the country. In some cases, the neighbors proved helpful, but in most they did not—in fact, they were often the source of many of Iraq's problems. Indeed, Iraq's neighbors have a much greater ability to cause harm to Iraq than to take constructive action that could genuinely help the country. For that reason, it is perhaps the best news of all that the influence of Iraq's neighbors is declining.

Iraqis are fiercely nationalistic and tend to dislike their neighbors. Consequently, as the Iraqi state has begun to regain its strength, it has inevitably begun to push back against the interference of virtually all of its neighbors. This has been clearly apparent with regard to Iran. In 2008, the Maliki government deliberately ignored Iranian wishes and sent the ISF into al-Basrah, Sadr City, al-Amarah, al-Qurnah, and several other cities to clear out Muqtada as-Sadr's Iranian-backed Jaysh al-Mahdi. Since then, Baghdad has also pushed back against other neighbors; it has regularly taken Damascus to task for allowing terrorists to cross Syria to sneak into Iraq and cause mayhem. Iraqi leaders have also begun to complain of Kuwaiti and Saudi recalcitrance.

Thus, as long as Iraq continues to progress toward becoming strong, stable, and unified, the more difficult it will be for its neighbors to dominate or destabilize it. Of course, the neighbors know this too and they—particularly Iran, but possibly Kuwait and Saudi Arabia as well—may still want to prevent Iraq from becoming too strong, in order to keep it from becoming a threat.

Yet in this area as well, it is important to recognize that there are many things that the Iraqi government desperately wants to see happen that hold relatively little interest for the United States. For instance, it is vital to Iraqi leaders to have Iraq removed from various UN Security Council dictates pursuant to Chapter VII of the UN Charter—which were initiated in 1990–1991 by the United Nations Security Council (UNSC) to deal with the problems created by Saddam Husayn's aggression. It matters relatively little to the United States whether Iraq is relieved of its Chapter VII restrictions or not. There are a range of such actions in the diplomatic arena that are very important to Baghdad and that Iraq probably cannot effect without significant American assistance. In every such case, these should be seen as yet another element of American influence and leverage in Iraq, and particularly a means of shaping the crucial crucible of Iraqi domestic politics.

Iraq in a Regional Context

An effective American strategy for drawing down the U.S. commitment to Iraq without pushing Iraq into civil war should consciously recognize the role of Iraq's neighbors either to help or hurt that process. It cannot be a simple bilateral process in conception or in implementation. Moreover, the United States must develop an integrated regional strategy that will assist with this transition by recognizing what Washington needs from the rest of the region when it comes to Iraq.

There is, however, a danger involved in this as well. Washington should move very cautiously when it comes to pressing Iraq into an explicitly pro-American, anti-Iranian coalition, for instance. Because Iraq remains weak and divided, it will likely require considerable diplomatic capital to push Iraq in this direction. At the very least, that means squandering the ability to influence Iraqi domestic politics on those matters of ultimately greater concern to the United States, like preventing a civil war. Over the long term, a strong Iraq will inevitably serve as a formidable obstacle to Iran, and if Iraq sees the American role as having been a positive one, it is likely to remain well-disposed toward Washington.

The Utility of a New Regional Security Architecture

As part of an American effort to help Iraq deal with its economic, diplomatic, and military issues within the Persian Gulf region, it would be useful to anchor the new Iraq in a wider regional structure. This structure should provide non-violent mechanisms to address security problems, and be a tangible sign to both Iraqis and their neighbors that Iraq has resumed its place as a sovereign member of the community of nations and is no longer a battleground to be contested. This is not the place for a full exposition of what a new security architecture for the Gulf region could or should entail.[1] However, because it could be an extremely important vehicle for the United States to advance its interests by routinizing and institutionalizing the strategic interactions of Iraq and its neighbors, it does deserve mention.

The United States should work with Iraq and its GCC allies along two parallel tracks. The first would be a revised alliance system that would bring Iraq and the United States into a new multilateral security relationship with the GCC states, and possibly with Egypt and Jordan as well. The goal would be to create a security structure with standing military-to-military relationships, including joint training and exercises, officer exchanges, joint planning, and command-and-control networking. At some point it might include formal provisions for mutual defense and even the stationing of troops on one another's soil. The goal would be to frame a more formal military arrangement that included Iraq, the United States, and the GCC states, thereby helping to legitimate the American military presence, grounding Iraq more formally in diplomatic and security ties with the GCC states, and bolstering the likelihood that a potential aggressor would not be able to divide and conquer.

The second track would be a broader security organization for the region that should include not only Iraq, the United States, and the GCC, but also Iran and possibly other great powers as well— ideally the other four permanent members of the UNSC. Such an organization would provide Iran, Iraq, and the GCC the opportunity to discuss their security concerns and hopefully address them by non-violent means. It could start with a regular series of meetings at which all member states would send representatives to discuss various security issues—both immediate and long standing. Over time, these conversations might lead to confidence-building measures, followed by security agreements, and eventually arms control and reduction treaties. One possible analogy is to how the Organization for Security and Cooperation in Europe (OSCE) evolved in a similar fashion during the last decades of the Cold War.

IRAQ AND ITS NEIGHBORS

The following is an overview of the interests of Iraq's neighbors and the measures that should be taken to ensure that they do not impede U.S. interests.

Kuwait

Although, as stated, Iraq's per capita GDP in 2009 amounted to only $3,800 (160th in the world) while Kuwait's stood at $54,100 (7th in the world), Kuwait continues to receive an annual payment of 5 percent of Iraqi oil revenues as reparations for Saddam's 1990 invasion and occupation.[2] With some justification, Iraq argues that the Iraqi people should not be held complicit indefinitely for Saddam Husayn's sins. Similarly, in demarcating the border after the Persian Gulf War, Iraq asserts that the UN effectively hemmed in

Iraq's second port of Umm Qasr (one of only two it possesses), making it impossible for ships to pass up the Khawr Abdallah waterway and disembark there without passing through Kuwaiti territorial waters. This too is a situation requiring remedy, probably in the form of an agreement between Kuwait and Iraq governing transit along the Khawr Abdallah to Umm Qasr, as part of a broader deal that includes Iraq reconfirming its adherence to UN resolutions on outstanding issues between the two countries.[3]

Like others in the region, the Kuwaitis are concerned about Iraq's future and have so far refused to negotiate on either the reparations or port issues because they see them as leverage over Iraq. Ultimately, the United States will have to broker a deal between Kuwait and Iraq because only the United States has the influence with both states to press them to make the necessary concessions and find ways to reward them for those compromises. Yet, a frequent complaint of senior Iraqi officials and diplomats is that since 2003, the U.S. government has made virtually no effort to address Iraq's disputes with Kuwait. This is something that the United States should address at some point on behalf of Iraq (and Kuwait), but only in return for Iraqi agreement on issues of importance to the United States. Alternatively, it is a step that Washington could undertake relatively quickly after a new government is formed in Baghdad as a way of giving the new Iraqi leadership a quick diplomatic "win" which could buy it some time to tackle Iraq's daunting economic, political, and bureaucratic problems.

Saudi Arabia

Since 2003, Saudi Arabia has been a source of frustration for Washington and Baghdad. Riyadh has steadfastly refused to take actions that could be helpful to Iraq. It has withheld diplomatic recognition, let alone diplomatic support. It has done little to encourage Saudi investment and trade with Iraq, and has committed relatively paltry amounts of aid. In addition, the Saudis have not made an effort to curb the flow of terrorists traveling to Iraq. Indeed, the Saudi government has generally treated Iraqi Prime Minister Nuri al-Maliki like a pariah.

Many Saudis claim that their antipathy is entirely directed at Maliki himself, but there is reason to be dubious of this claim. Saudis will openly say that they cannot and will not countenance Shi'ah dominance of Iraq, whether it is Maliki or someone else. Indeed, Saudi Arabia poured money into Iraq during the 2010 election campaign, backing every Sunni group as well as 'Ayad Allawi's secular Iraqiyya Party. Although Allawi is a Shi'ah, he has long been considered acceptable by Sunnis in and out of Iraq, and much of his electoral support was drawn from Iraq's Sunni tribal community—the Iraqi groups closest to Saudi Arabia.

Saudi policy toward Iraq exacerbates the flaws in Iraq's domestic politics that could bring about a new civil war. The Saudis see their financial support to Iraq's Sunnis as a counterweight to Iran's financial support to various Shi'i groups. This situation risks enabling those voices in the Iraqi Sunni community who argue that the Shi'ah will never give them equal power in the central government and therefore Iraq's Sunni-dominated provinces should either cease cooperation with the central government or actively oppose it through a return to insurgency.

Moreover, as the de facto leader of the Arab world, Saudi Arabia's unwillingness to accept Iraq back into the Arab fold could force Baghdad into the arms of Tehran. This is not inevitable: the vast majority of Iraq's Shi'ah, including all of the current major leaders, would prefer to keep the Iranians at arm's length, and ultimately see themselves first as Arab Iraqis, not Shi'ah. Famously, the Iraqi Shi'ah did not rise up in revolt against Saddam during the Iran-Iraq war, as Khomeini had expected, because they hated the Persians more than Saddam. Despite this, since 2003, Shi'i leaders in Iraq have been consistently forced to demonstrate to the Iraqi electorate that they are not beholden to Iran. Yet if Iraq is left with no alternative, it will turn to Tehran by default.

Consequently, Washington needs to make a major push to bring Riyadh around on Iraq. Washington will have to convince Riyadh that its fears are unfounded, and that the best way to avoid civil war in Iraq (Riyadh's worst nightmare) is to buttress the new Iraqi government, rather than undermine it. It may also mean bringing the Saudis into American and Iraqi counsels so that they can become comfortable with Iraq's leaders and their plans. A good vehicle for this, eventually, would be the regional security structures discussed above. In the near term, it might be helpful for Washington to broker a series of meetings among U.S., Iraqi, and Saudi officials to discuss Iraq's future course. Over time, this might even be expanded to a standing commission that could bring in other GCC countries as well, and expand its scope to address collective economic and political matters.

Iran

Iran continues to play a destabilizing role in Iraq. Iran suffered some critical defeats in the ousting of Muqtada as-Sadr's Jaysh al-Mahdi from al-Basrah and Sadr City in 2008, their failure to scuttle the U.S.-Iraq Security Agreement in 2008, and the defeat of their partisans in the 2009 provincial elections. But rather than quit the field, Iran's allies have simply changed their methods, and so retain considerable influence in Iraq. They continue to fund many Iraqi political parties, militias, and terrorist groups. They dominate Iraqi trade and its lucrative religious pilgrimage industry. They remain influential in Iraqi religious circles, and they have reminded Iraq that when the Americans finally leave, they can pose a serious military threat to Iraq.

Even if Iran's efforts do not help propel Iraq into civil war, they have the potential to produce a weak and divided Iraq subject to Iranian manipulation and domination. That is, after all, Iran's principal objective in Iraq. Such an outcome would be a very significant threat to American interests. It is also not something that the Iraqis or America's Arab allies would find desirable or even palatable. Indeed, it would greatly exacerbate fears of a new "Shi'i crescent" among many of the Sunni Arab states, and could well prompt them to take a range of precipitous and belligerent moves toward Iran that would be equally destabilizing for the region and deleterious to American interests.

The problem is that the United States has little ability to affect Iranian behavior directly. If that is the bad news about America's ability to influence Iranian activities, in the specific case of Iranian influence in Iraq, the United States has a critical ace in the hole that it lacks on every other policy issue with Iran: Iraqi nationalism. Because Iraqis generally do not like Persians and staunchly resist Iranian efforts to interfere in their affairs, Iraqi nationalism provides a "natural limit" on Iranian influence in Iraq, to quote former Ambassador Ryan Crocker. The stronger and more unified Iraq becomes, the more that Iraqis—Sunni, Shi'ah, and Kurd—will feel confident enough to push back on Iran. And the Iraqis can push back on Iranian activities in Iraq far better than the United States can, but Iraqi willingness to resist Iran's continued pressure—including military pressure—depends in part on the willingness of the U.S. to stand by Iraq in its struggle to remain independent of Tehran.

Turkey

In contrast to Saudi Arabia and Iran, Turkey has played a positive role in Iraq's affairs in recent years (with water issues an important exception). It has forged effective relations with both Baghdad and Irbil, which is a remarkable achievement given Turkish sensitivities. Consequently, the United States has a strong interest in seeing them continue.

So far, Turkey has been pursuing this course because Ankara sees it in its own interests to do so. This may not always be the case, however, and it would be useful for the United States to provide Turkey with some added incentives to stay this course. Elsewhere, Henri Barkey has described a range of steps that the United States could take to help cement Turkey's positive role in Iraq for the medium or even long term. These include:

—Pressing the KRG to extirpate the remnants of the terrorist Kurdistan Workers' Party (PKK) from northern Iraq, a critical security concern of the Turks.

—Pushing Iraq to ensure that its natural gas exports (when these finally come on line in several years) flow north through Turkey's Nabucco pipeline.

—Encouraging Baghdad to establish Qualified Industrial Zones between Turkey and Iraq (including Turkey and the KRG) to promote trade and create jobs in both countries.

—Including Turkish officials more regularly in conversations with Iraq to reassure Ankara and secure Turkish "buy-in" for Iraqi policies.[4]

In addition, the United States should encourage Iraq and Turkey to reach agreement on an equitable arrangement for water management.

Syria

Iraq has critical long-term issues with Syria over water rights, the return and status of Iraqi refugees, and a variety of other matters. However, Baghdad's most pressing problem with Damascus is Syria's continued willingness to allow small numbers of Salafi terrorists to cross Syrian territory to Iraq, where they are often the deadliest of the remaining terrorists still plaguing the country. The Iraqi regime believes that many of the worst bombings they have experienced since 2008 have been perpetrated by figures who crossed into Iraq from Syria.

The problem is that Syria's principal target seems to be Washington more than Baghdad. The Syrians seek a rapprochement with the United States, a grand bargain in which they would get a peace treaty with Israel that met all of their needs in Lebanon and the Golan Heights, along with American economic support. The Syrians seem to regard the flow of foreign fighters into Iraq (which they have reduced over the years) to be a source of leverage in that effort: it is a chit to be traded to the United States in return for getting the deal they want. Thus, Iraq's problem with Syria is ultimately America's problem with Syria.

NOTES

CHAPTER ONE

1. President Barack Obama, "Remarks at the Disabled American Veterans National Convention," August 2, 2010.

2. See for instance, Paul Collier and Anke Hoeffler, "Greed and Grievance in Civil War," The World Bank Development Research Group, Policy Research Working Paper 2355, 2000; James D. Fearon, "Primary Commodity Exports and Civil War," *Journal of Conflict Resolution* 49, no. 4 (2005), pp. 483–507; James D. Fearon and David Laitin, "Ethnicity, Insurgency, and Civil War," *American Political Science Review* 97, no. 1 (February 2003), pp. 75–90; James D. Fearon and David Laitin, "Violence and the Social Construction of Ethnic Identity," *International Organization* 54, no. 4 (2002), pp. 845–877; James D. Fearon, "Why Do Some Civil Wars Last So Much Longer than Others?" *Journal of Peace Research* 41, no. 3 (May 2004), pp. 275–302; T. David Mason, "Sustaining the Peace after Civil War," The Strategic Studies Institute, U.S. Army War College, Carlisle, PA, December 2007; Michael Ross, "What Do We Know about Natural Resources and Civil War?" *Journal of Peace Research*, May 2004; Nicholas Sambanis, "A Review of Recent Advances and Future Directions in the Literature on Civil War," *Defense and Peace Economics* 13, no. 2 (2002): Barbara Walter and Jack Snyder, eds., *Civil Wars, Insecurity, and Intervention* (New York: Columbia University Press, 1999); Barbara Walter, "Does Conflict Beget Conflict? Explaining Recurring Civil War," *Journal of Peace Research* 41, no. 3 (May 2004), pp. 371–388.

3. On the effects and impact of civil wars on neighboring states see Daniel L. Byman and Kenneth M. Pollack, *Things Fall Apart: Containing the Spillover from an Iraqi Civil War* (Washington, DC: The Brookings Institution Press, 2007).

4. Walter and Snyder, eds., *Civil Wars, Insecurity, and Intervention*; Walter, "Does Conflict Beget Conflict?" pp. 371–388.

5. "Iraqis Say 'Wrong Time' for U.S. Withdrawal: Poll," Agence France-Presse, August 24, 2010.

6. Liz Sly, "Iraq Needs Help Defending Its Borders after U.S. Troops Leave in 2011," *Los Angeles Times*, August 12, 2010.

7. The Security Agreement (SA) is often erroneously referred to as a "status of forces agreement (SOFA)." The SA serves a similar purpose, but the Iraqis specifically objected to naming it a "SOFA" because of the negative connotations associated with that term in Middle Eastern, particularly Iranian, history.

Chapter Two

1. "State of Law Official Supports the Establishment of Federalism in Southern Iraq and Criticizes Opponents," *Nakheel News*, October 27, 2010; "Basra to Demand Turning into a Region," *Aswat al-Iraq*, September 5, 2010.

2. See the "Political Reform Document" adopted by the Council of Representatives along with the Security Agreement on November 27, 2008.

3. It is worth noting that constitutional reform and development is not fully synonymous with constitutional amendments. There are a host of laws mandated by the Constitution in areas as diverse as ensuring the independence of the judiciary, functioning of the cabinet, and oil and revenue sharing that have not been passed and if adopted could significantly help to ameliorate constitutional ambiguities.

4. See comments by international comparative constitutional expert Yash Ghai, who has serious reservations as to "whether the constitution as it stands can be fully and effectively implemented without grave danger to state and society," quoted in Jonathan Morrow, "Iraq's Constitutional Process II: An Opportunity Lost," USIP Special Report No. 155, November 2005. Commentary by the International Crisis Group argues that: "Instead of healing the growing divisions between Iraq's three principal communities—Shiites, Kurds and Sunni Arabs—a rushed constitutional process has deepened rifts and hardened feelings." It goes on to say that key passages on decentralization are "vague and ambiguous so as to sow the seeds of future discord." International Crisis Group, "Unmaking Iraq: A Constitutional Process Gone Awry," Middle East Briefing No. 19, September 2005.

5. For example, in an unusual arrangement, the prime minister cannot dismiss members of his own cabinet. The Constitution gives Parliament the power not just to withdraw its confidence in the government as a whole but also from ministers on an individual basis. In a further practice uncommon to parliamentary

systems, the prime minister can only recommend the dissolution of Parliament and new elections—it is the legislature itself which has the final decision on dissolving itself.

6. See United States Institute of Peace, "Iraq's Federal Executive: Options for Executive Power Sharing," November 2008, which is the source for some the options below.

7. This option highlights a separate but related issue of the importance of the independence of the Federal Supreme Court (FSC) and that Iraqis have not yet implemented constitutional requirements to pass laws fully establishing the administrative and financial independence of the FSC or the Higher Judicial Council, the latter being the body responsible for administrative oversight of the entire judiciary.

8. Enhancing the powers of the president, rather than having this position remain largely ceremonial, could actually increase this problem, again suggesting the need for direct election of the president.

9. Alternatively, given that the largest bloc may not even approach a majority, the Constitution could ask the president to propose a nominee who in his view holds the support of a majority of members. This would make it clear that coalition building rather than strict order of finish in the elections is most important and place an emphasis on developing a government program that can obtain the support of other groups.

CHAPTER THREE

1. For instance, see "Iraqis Say 'Wrong Time' for US Withdrawal: Poll," Agence France-Presse, August 24, 2010.

2. For more on this phenomenon, see Kenneth M. Pollack and Irena L. Sargsyan, "The Other Side of the COIN: The Perils of Premature Evacuation from Iraq," *The Washington Quarterly* 33, no. 2 (April 2010), pp. 17–32.

3. Lourdes Garcia-Navarro, "As U.S. Troops Depart, Some Iraqis Fear Their Own," National Public Radio, June 21, 2010, available at <http://www.npr.org/templates/story/story.php?storyId=127986221&ft=1&f=1001>, accessed on October 9, 2010.

4. See Kenneth M. Pollack, *Arabs at War: Military Effectiveness, 1948-1991* (Lincoln, NE: University of Nebraska Press, 2002).

CHAPTER FOUR

1. United Nations Office for the Coordination of Humanitarian Affairs, Inter-Agency Information and Analysis Unit, "Iraq Labour Force Analysis 2003–2008," January 2009.

2. With our thanks to Robert Cassily for this simple, eloquent conceptualization of the primary challenge.

3. Transparency International ranked Iraq ranked 175th out of the 178 countries surveyed in its 2010 corruption perceptions index. Transparency International, Corruptions Perceptions Index 2010, October 26, 2010, available at <http://www.transparency.org/policy_research/surveys_indices/cpi/2010/results>.

4. International Monetary Fund, "Iraq: Staff Report for the 2009 Article IV Consultation and Request for Stand-By Arrangement," March 2010. According to this report, only slightly over one-third (38 percent) of the Iraqi population is officially employed (mostly in the public sector) and almost half of total household income is provided by the government.

5. The U.S. has already appropriated almost $54 billion for Iraqi reconstruction since 2003, expended over 90 percent of this money, and is unlikely to make significant new appropriations. Special Inspector General for Iraq Reconstruction (SIGIR), *Quarterly Report and Semi-Annual Report to the U.S. Congress*, July 30, 2010. SIGIR estimates that even if existing requests from the Administration for FY 10 and FY 11 are fully funded by Congress, U.S. reconstruction funds will largely be expended sometime in 2011.

6. As discussed in the section Regional Issues.

7. An estimated 22 percent of Iraq's electricity generation capacity is from hydropower. U.S. Energy Information Administration, *Country Analysis Briefs, Iraq*, August 2007. The production of a barrel of oil requires around 1.6 barrels of water. Serena Chaudry, "Lack of Water Threatens Iraq's Long-Term Stability," Reuters, June 6, 2010. Of course, water for oil injection can be saline, but Iraq's infrastructure is currently designed to draw only from freshwater sources for oil field injection. Consequently, Iraq would at the very least need to build a new network to bring seawater north to the oil fields to compensate for diminished freshwater.

8. Middle East Economic Survey, "Interview: Iraqi Minister of Water Resources," *Energy and Geopolitical Risk* 1, no. 1, February 2010. BCM figures come from a table in the same article sourced to: Republic of Iraq Ministry of Water Resources, Water Resources Development Strategies, Baghdad, 2010.

9. Phil Sands and Nizar Latif, "Iraq's New War Is a Fight for Water," *The National*, September 4, 2009.

10. Joel Whitaker and Anand Varghese, "The Tigris-Euphrates River Basin: A Science Diplomacy Opportunity," USIP PeaceBrief No. 20, April 22, 2010.

11. UNESCO, *Survey of Infiltration Karez in Northern Iraq: History and Current Status of Underground Aqueducts*, IQ/2009/SC/RP/1, September 2009.

12. "Iraq: Killing for Water," IRIN, June 23, 2010.

13. Ibid.

14. In May 2009, the Iraqi Parliament refused to approve a free trade agreement with Turkey until the agreement contained a provision guaranteeing Iraq's share of the Tigris and Euphrates. The Parliament also passed a law saying that

the water issue should be raised by the Iraqi government in all meetings between the two countries.

15. In 2003, the World Bank estimated that the agricultural sector accounted for 8 percent of GDP but 20 percent of employment in Iraq. A 2006 FAO report estimated that the agriculture sector employed 37 percent of the workforce. The most recent COSIT figures indicate that as of 2008 the sector had declined to 4 percent of GDP from 9 percent in 2003.

16. SIGIR, *Quarterly Report and Semi-Annual Report to the U.S. Congress*, January 30 2010. See the report on the Comparison of GOI Budgets, 2007–2010, pg. 19. In 2010, $2.18 billion was allocated for provincial investment funds.

17. Budget execution, defined as the release of funds from the federal government to the provincial councils, rather than actual disbursement for projects, increased from 34 percent to 91 percent from 2007 to 2009.

18. Rusty Barber and Sam Parker, "Evaluating Iraq's Provincial Reconstruction Teams While Drawdown Looms," USIP Trip Report, United States Institute of Peace, December 2008.

19. PPAT was implemented by Grant Thornton and facilitated budget implementation by subcontracting with Iraqi companies to establish procurement assistance teams in each governorate and in the Office of Government Public Contracting Policy at the Ministry of Planning and Development in Baghdad (the Ministry plays a key role approving the release of funds). The PPAT program was unique because there was a substantial financial motivation for the provincial officials to ensure that the PPAT team was effective. The PPAT team was essentially responsible for ensuring that the governor's and provincial council's chosen capital projects were approved by the Ministry of Planning and the Ministry of finance, and the funds were subsequently released.

CHAPTER FIVE

1. For a fuller discussion of this topic, see Joseph McMillan, "The United States and a Gulf Security Architecture: Policy Considerations," *Strategic Insights* 3, no. 3 (March 2004); Kenneth M. Pollack, "Securing the Gulf," *Foreign Affairs* 82, no. 4 (July–August 2003), pp. 2–16; James A. Russell, "Searching for a Post-Saddam Regional Security Architecture," *Middle East Review of International Affairs (MERIA)* 7, no. 1 (March, 2003).

2. This level of reparations is set by the United Nations Security Council and has been successively reduced from 30 percent to 25 percent, and then to the current level.

3. In particular UN Security Council Resolution 833, which Kuwaitis see as symbolic in terms of Iraq respecting its existence.

4. Henri Barkey, "Turkey's New Engagement in Iraq: Embracing Iraqi Kurdistan," USIP Special Report 237, United States Institute of Peace, May 2010, pp. 14–16.

About the Authors

KENNETH M. POLLACK is the Director of the Saban Center for Middle East Policy and a Senior Fellow at Brookings. He served as the Director of Research of the Saban Center from 2002 to 2009. He has served as Director for Persian Gulf Affairs and Near East and South Asian Affairs at the National Security Council, Senior Research Professor at National Defense University, and Persian Gulf military analyst at the CIA. His latest book is *A Path out of the Desert: A Grand Strategy for America in the Middle East* (Random House). He is also the author of *The Persian Puzzle: The Conflict between Iran and America* (Random House), *The Threatening Storm: The Case for Invading Iraq* (Random House), and *Arabs at War: Military Effectiveness, 1948–1991* (University of Nebraska Press).

RAAD ALKADIRI is a Partner and Head of Global Risk at PFC Energy, the Washington-based strategic advisory firm. A country risk specialist, he leads PFC Energy's Iraq Advisory practice. He previously served as Policy Advisor and Assistant Private Secretary to the UK Special Representatives to Iraq from 2003 to 2004, and Senior Policy Advisor to Her Majesty's Ambassador in Baghdad from 2006 to 2007. Prior to joining PFC Energy in 1998, he was Deputy Managing Editor at the U.K.-based consultancy Oxford Analytica. He was a member of the Economy and Reconstruction Expert Working Group for the Baker-Hamilton Commission and a member of the Council on Foreign Relations/James A. Baker III Institute for Public Policy of Rice University Independent Work Group on Guiding Principles for U.S. Post-Conflict Policy in Iraq. He is also a founder-member of the Arab Energy Club.

J. SCOTT CARPENTER is the Keston Family Fellow at the Washington Institute for Near East Policy and Director of Project Fikra, a program focusing on empowering Arab democrats in their struggle against authoritarianism and extremism. He served previously as Deputy Assistant Secretary of State in the Bureau of Near East Affairs from 2004 to 2007 and was named Coordinator of the Broader Middle East and North Africa Initiative in 2006. From April 2003 to June 2004, he served as Director of the Governance Group in the Coalition Provisional Authority in Baghdad. He is author of *Views of Arab Democrats: Advice to America on Promoting Middle East Reform*. His most recent publication, *Fighting the Ideological Battle: The Missing Link in U.S. Strategy to Counter Violent Extremism*, was coauthored with Dr. Matthew Levitt.

FREDERICK W. KAGAN is a Resident Scholar at the American Enterprise Institute. He is a former professor of military history at the U.S. Military Academy at West Point. He is the author of the 2007 report *Choosing Victory: A Plan for Success in Iraq*, and was one of the intellectual architects of the "surge" strategy in Iraq. His books include *Ground Truth: The Future of U.S. Land Power* (AEI Press, 2008), coauthored with Thomas Donnelly, and *End of the Old Order: Napoleon and Europe, 1801–1805* (Da Capo, 2006).

SEAN KANE is the senior Program Officer for Iraq at the United States Institute of Peace (USIP). He assists in the management of the Institute's Iraq program and field mission in Iraq, and serves as USIP's primary expert on Iraq and U.S. policy in Iraq. He worked with the United Nations Assistance Mission in Iraq (UNAMI) from 2006 to 2009, where he advised the Iraqi Parliament, monitored elections and helped to prepare UNAMI's reports on Kirkuk and other disputed internal boundaries. He has published on the subjects of Iraqi politics and natural resource negotiations, including "Iraq's Oil Politics: Where Agreement Might Be Found" (USIP Peaceworks, January 2010).

Index

Abu Dhabi, 92–93
Accountability, transparency and oversight: Iraqi people's desire for, 37; of
  oil economy, 89, 95–96; in provincial
  governance, 104; U.S. aid conditioned on, 10, 90, 92
Afghanistan, 20
Agency for International Development
  (USAID), 103, 104
Agricultural sector, 89, 96, 99–100
Aid and assistance from U.S.: conditional provision of, 3–4, 6, 9, 10,
  33–34, 39–40, 89–90, 92, 100;
  current scope of, 31; future pros-
  pects for, 90–91; to Iraqi military,
  27, 79–82; Iraqi perception of, 17,
  25–26; for Iraq's integration into
  international economy, 28; limitations to, 10; provincial governance
  and, 103–04; rationale, 32; recom-
  mendations for, 3–4, 10, 90; as
  source of U.S. influence in Iraq,
  31–32, 33–34; Strategic Framework
  Agreement for, 31–32, 90–92; to
  strengthen Iraq's diplomatic relations, 27–28; U.S. military presence

to protect, 69–70; for water manage-
  ment, 100
Allawi, Ayad, 44, 110
Al-Qa'ida, 63, 74, 76–77
Anbar, 42
Asymmetric federalism, 52–53
Attachment claims, 95–96
Awakening movement, 64

Barkey, Henri, 112
Basrah, 42, 43, 52, 103
Ba'ath Party, 51, 67; de-Ba'athification
  campaign, 43, 44
Bosnia, 15
Bush (G. W.) administration, 17, 29, 65,
  85, 87

Civil service, 41
Civil war in Iraq: conditions favoring,
  18–19; disorganized U.S. exit contributing to risk of, 16–17; implica-
  tions for future of Iraq, 15; potential
  for, 1, 15, 19; regional destabiliza-
  tion from, 18, 19–20; role of U.S. in
  preventing, 7–8, 15, 18–20; threat to
  U.S. interests from, 2, 15